Classroom Strategies

for Effective Early Education

purposeful design®
p u b l i c a t i o n s

Colorado Springs, Colorado

D'Arcy Maher, Editor

Purposeful Design Publications is the publishing division of the Association of Christian Schools International (ACSI) and is committed to the ministry of Christian school education, to enable Christian educators and schools worldwide to effectively prepare students for life. As the publisher of textbooks, trade books, and other educational resources within ACSI, Purposeful Design Publications strives to produce biblically sound materials that reflect Christian scholarship and stewardship and that address the identified needs of Christian schools around the world.

Unless otherwise identified, all Scripture quotations are taken from the Holy Bible, New International Version©. Copyright © 1973, 1978, 1984 by Biblica, Inc. All rights reserved worldwide. Used by permission.

Scripture quotations marked (NASB) are taken from the New American Standard Bible. Copyright © 1960, 1962, 1963, 1968, 1971, 1972, 1973, 1975, 1977, 1995 by The Lockman Foundation. Used by permission.

Scripture quotations marked (NKJV) are taken from the Holy Bible, New King James Version (NKJV). Copyright © 1982 by Thomas Nelson, Inc. Used by permission. All rights reserved.

Printed in the United States of America
19 18 17 16 15 14 13 12 11   1 2 3 4 5 6 7

Maher, D'Arcy, editor
    Classroom strategies for effective early education
    ISBN 978-1-58331-380-0   Catalog #6635

Design team: Bethany Kerstetter, Mike Riester
Editorial team: Gina Brandon, Cheryl Chiapperino

Purposeful Design Publications
A Division of ACSI
PO Box 65130 • Colorado Springs CO 80962-5130
Customer Service: 800-367-0798 • www.acsi.org

This compilation of *Christian Early Education* (CEE) magazine articles was created to support your intentional practices as you work with and nurture young children.

We in ACSI Early Education Services dedicate this book to you, the enthusiastic Christian early educators who nurture young children to the glory of God.

Contents

Section 5: Technology

Section 6: Bonus Articles

Introduction

Why Another Early Education Book?

Intentional practices. *Intentionality* is perhaps one of the loveliest words in the English language. It encompasses *purpose*, *planning*, *meaningfulness*, *nuance*, *creativity*, and *capacity*. Its opposites, such as *chance* and *accident*, clarify the definition even more. When we bring the beauty of this word into the early education classroom, teaching practices elevate the experience of the child. Learning occurs and growth emerges.

Distinctly Christian programs. Those programs that chose to include a faith distinctive enjoy the unfettered opportunity to integrate and celebrate the life of Christ and the words of Scripture throughout the entire program. Does your program embrace this reality? Does your team strive to know Christ and make Him known throughout every part of the day?

Perhaps this book will breathe new life and excitement into your endeavors to create a program that is even more distinctly Christian.

A common language: ministry. There is no dearth of quality early education resources. The field is blessed with competent and capable authors on many topics. We applaud their work.

Our commitment to you, however, is to approach each topic from a distinctly biblical worldview and to share any message in our common language: ministry to children and families. This common focus binds us together in a passionate commitment to this ministry. Will you explore this book, written in the language of ministry, with your team?

Careful stewardship. Over the years, we have been blessed to have exemplary practitioners and academicians write for *Christian Early Education* magazine. Because the magazine is a cornerstone of the ACSI Early Education Department, we sometimes overlook the fact that this piece often fails to reach classroom teachers and teacher assistants.

As stewards of this archive, we've compiled relevant, topical articles that are accessible to any early educator—without the barrier of a subscription. We've enriched the offerings and added a CD of rich resources.

Wander among the pages. Download the resources. Enjoy!

Essential Beliefs of ACSI Early Education

Children are a gift from God. Procreation is an awesome privilege and responsibility, and it is God's provision for the continuation of humankind. Rather than seeing a statistic, we view each child as a gift with talents, potential, and purpose. Each child is carefully crafted by God; parents welcome, protect, and pray for their children and introduce them to the world in which they all live. Parents serve as stewards of the gift of their children.

Psalms 139:13–16,127:3–5

Parents are children's primary teachers. God lovingly gives children to parents, who serve as the children's first teachers by coaching the children in self-care (feeding, walking, bathing, etc.), introducing them to their environment, and providing an example of basic living skills. Throughout children's lives, parents retain responsibility for them and serve as their primary influences and teachers, whether positive or negative. Scripture validates this role by providing clear instructions on how parents should intentionally guide children.

Deuteronomy 4:9, 6:4–9; Psalm 78:5–6

Changing family structures provide rich opportunities for ministry. God's intent for a family consists of a godly father and a godly mother equally committed to raising their children. Reality, however, reminds us of the many single-parent homes, of adopted children, and of children raised by extended family, by guardians in foster care, in families that reflect postmodern cultural extremes, and by parents who are detached and disengaged. We remember that God loves each individual intensely, that the gospel message reflects God's heart of redemption, and that we are to be salt and light in a dark world.

Romans 5:8, Luke 4:14–21, Matthew 5:13–16

Quality early education programs support the success of children and families. Children bear the consequences of the decisions of their parents, whether positive or negative. Children cannot be held accountable for their parents' decisions; consequently, Christian early educators should not show favoritism to a child from an advantaged setting or judgment to a child from a disadvantaged setting. Rather, Christian early education programs strive to intersect with the lives of children and families in the same way that Christ would if He were serving in that program. Christian early education programs can support families through a wealth of resources by providing parent training, connecting families to valuable programs in local churches, or referring families to organizations within the program's wide faith-based network. Because they recognize that God places the responsibility for a child on the parents, Christian early educators partner with parents and guardians for the benefit of the child.

Luke 19:10, 2 Corinthians 2:14–15, Galatians 6:2, 9–10

Christ's example and His teaching on children must infuse every interaction. Christ's attention to children provides a glimpse into the heart of God. Though small and vulnerable, children represent the kingdom of God, and we are to become like them. Christ welcomed children, blessed them, advocated for them to disapproving adults, pronounced judgment on those who would cause them to sin, and identified them as those who exemplify greatness in the kingdom.

Mark 9:33–37, 42; Matthew 18:1–6, 10; Matthew 19:13–15

Essential Values of ACSI Early Education

Dynamic, authentic expressions of biblical principles. The design of all activities and experiences (the whole of what happens in the program) begins with the intent of integrating the truths of Scripture into every aspect of the program. Do all routines, transitions, mealtimes, exploration activities, and instruction support the emergence of biblical principles and teachable moments? Biblical principles become living principles when they are expressed in the lives of teachers and not isolated within the curriculum.

The value of all children. Every child is a unique and special creation from the hand of God. Children in a community of learners gain appreciation for children of different cultures, genders, and abilities as a result of the value that the adults in program leadership place on each child.

The value of the early childhood years. Child development is a unique and complex process. Childhood, the journey through which children travel, is honored as a God-ordained process characterized by unique and distinct development; therefore, early education programs intentionally provide optimum learning experiences for the whole child—experiences that include spiritual, social, emotional, physical, and cognitive development. The process is meaningful.

The valued role of parents and family. Recognizing the importance of parents as the primary educators of their children, the early childhood program supports and intentionally encourages parent partnership in the educational and spiritual formation process.

The value of age-appropriate experiences. Just as God gave Jesus time to grow and develop, so we acknowledge that children need time to develop. Development is not hurried; neither is it left to chance. On the basis of Scripture and best practices, early educators intentionally plan experiences that will have great meaning at the age levels in each classroom.

The significance of accessibility. In Scripture, Jesus was accessible to children. The teacher-child relationship is the cornerstone of a successful early education experience. Early educators embrace their role in reflecting God's intense delight in children through quality interactions that are personal and individualized and that reflect deeply interested and sensitive adults.

The goal of serving disadvantaged families. Poverty reduces the choices of parents to meet the needs of their children in every area (e.g., health, lodging, nourishment, education) by limiting opportunities and alternatives. Throughout Scripture, care for those on the margins of society—the poor, the downtrodden, the immigrant, the orphan, the widow—is expected of believers. Early educators find creative ways to engage disadvantaged families and children, and they seek to mitigate the effects of poverty through fully trained staff members who are sensitive in planning and interactions as they address the needs of the community.

Section 1:
Curriculum Planning

Excellence in Early Education: What Is It?

By Milton Uecker. Reprinted from *CEE*, August 2007.

Best instructional practice for young children continues to be an unresolved issue in Christian schools. As recently as last fall I received an email about whether developmentally appropriate strategies were a legitimate consideration in the correspondent's school, and if so, what might these be. The concern was that the strategies would result in a dumbing down of the curriculum. The question came from an earnest desire to provide an effective program for young children, a program that does not compromise today's "high expectation" standards. How can we best teach the whole child in order to fully prepare him or her for a future that will demand not only the mastery of intellectual standards but also the curiosity, creativity, big-picture thinking, social competence, and love for learning that futurists predict will be highly valued in tomorrow's economy (Friedman 2006; Pink 2005)? What characterizes excellence in early education?

According to Thomas Armstrong in his book *The Best Schools: How Human Development Research Should Inform Educational Practice* (2006), the direction an educational program takes depends on its leadership's "discourse," or overarching way of thinking about education and the teaching and learning process. Armstrong identifies two dominant views, or discourses, that influence educational practices today. Academic achievement discourse, human development discourse, or both influence the classroom environment of a program, that program's daily practices, and ultimately its curriculum and expected outcomes. Contrasts within these belief systems often create a conflict because what we do in a classroom and what we believe about the nature and needs of the young child may not be in alignment.

Academic achievement discourse focuses on the cognitive, or academic, aspects of schooling. Standardized tests measure achievement, and educators use group norms to evaluate the results. The need for uniform rigorous standards and preparation for the future heavily influence the program's design and the children's educational experience (Armstrong 2006). The demands of the future push curriculum expectations downward.

3

In contrast, human development discourse "places the greatest emphasis on *human beings* rather than on *academics*" (Armstrong 2006, 36; italics in original). An emphasis on human development suggests a process involving the growth of the whole child across all strands of development: cognitive, emotional, social, physical, moral, and spiritual. Because children are on varying developmental timelines, instruction is flexible and more individualized. Evaluation methods focus on each child and measure an individual child's growth over time (Armstrong 2006).

As educators whose worldview is biblical, we address issues and view life from the perspective of a biblical discourse. At age 12, Jesus demonstrated an amazing understanding of the Scriptures, and He was able to question the most learned rabbis (Luke 2:46–47). Even though Jesus showed a high level of cognitive maturity, God had a view that focused on His Son's total development. "Jesus kept increasing in wisdom and stature, and in favor with God and men (Luke 2:52, NASB). In His ministry, Jesus—unlike the Pharisees, whose expectations were group or norm based—focused on individuals. He met and taught people according to their needs and background. Paul offered the Corinthians "milk to drink, not solid food" because their spiritual immaturity prevented them from understanding teaching at higher levels (1 Corinthians 3:2). Children speak, think, and reason like children (1 Corinthians 13:11). Cognitively they are immature. This immaturity is no doubt the reason why their instruction, according to Deuteronomy 6:7, must be through modeling (work on the heart of the teacher first) and life experience throughout the day as opposed to a more formal didactic approach. God is concerned about academic achievement, but likewise, He wants caregivers to view cognitive growth as part of the whole and to bring it about in a way that respects childhood and the fact that children can be easily made to "stumble" (Matthew 18:6).

Perhaps it is the knowledge of these truths that creates so much conflict for Christian early educators. On the one hand we face increasingly higher and higher academic expectations, while at the same time knowing that children are often not ready for the tasks at hand. We may change expectations and the nature of our outcomes in the context of a changing world, but young children are still children, whose nature and needs remain the same.

To establish a foundation for our curriculum, we must know about the nature of young children and examine our beliefs regarding how they learn. Young children are integrated and immature individuals, and they need involvement, social interaction, and moral instruction.

Individuals

All children are uniquely created on an individual developmental timetable, and each one has a different experiential and cultural background. They have wonderfully different genetic blueprints, learning styles, and talents. Their development is uneven. Though they may excel cognitively, as often evidenced by their oral language, they may be delayed physically, socially, or emotionally. Early experiences influence readiness and brain development, and these experiences are different in every home. Educators must address these variances in each child as well as in the group.

Integrated

Each child must be viewed as an integrated whole (Luke 2:52). Growth in one area—whether cognitive, social, emotional, spiritual, or physical—is dependent on and integrated with growth in other areas. An overemphasis in one may take place at the cost of timely development in another. Young children must learn to move and move to learn, and this learning results in a greater capacity to think. For example, a preschooler's social and emotional skill development is dependent on interactions with real people (Jensen 2005). In turn, the nature of these interactions changes, and it is enhanced by the child's physical growth and language development.

Immature

Children are all in the process of growing; therefore, their teachers must evaluate and accommodate children's readiness for a given skill. Because children think and speak like children (1 Corinthians 13:11), content must begin with concepts that are in the scope of the children's past experience and present understanding. Educators must avoid making assumptions about children's essential prior experiences and

5

prerequisite skills. Therefore, early educators have the task of thinking in terms of activities that promote growth and readiness as opposed to instruction that is dependent on an unrealistic level of cognitive and physical maturity.

Involvement

Learning takes place through sensory involvement and immersion in each concept. As children are exposed to and interact with concrete, firsthand experiences, their minds form mental models that are necessary for understanding and future learning (Jensen 2005). If thinking is the goal, active processing must be the means. Early education is therefore often noisy and messy. Children learn by encountering lots of stuff located in carefully designed spaces.

Social Interaction

Learning must take place in a community of learners where thoughts are clarified and exchanged through verbal interactions with teachers and more competent peers. The language of children symbolically represents what they are experiencing and understanding. Clear and accurate oral expression by children validates their learning. Play provides dynamic opportunities not only to demonstrate and practice new concepts and vocabulary but also to develop social skills (Jensen 2005). Thus, a well-designed playground and well-designed classroom activity centers are comparable to well-equipped high school science labs.

Moral Instruction

Young children need to learn to respect (honor) and obey in order to grow in Christlikeness (Ephesians 6:1–3). All learning takes discipline, and the will and attitudes are influenced early in life (Proverbs 22:6). Children must learn rules of conduct and the behaviors that are appropriate in school. "The child's respect for [parental] authority is the single most important moral legacy that comes out of the child's relations with the parent" (Damon 1988, 52). The teacher's authority and the school's rules of conduct are likewise essential to the classroom's functioning. Thus, respecting the teacher and obeying his or her rules contributes to children's moral growth. Educators must therefore view time spent in teaching behavioral expectations and responding to children's inappropriate behavior as integral to, as opposed to a distraction from, the curriculum.

How do these principles, applied together, shape an early education classroom? Teachers focus on the children. They study child development, both formally and through observation over time, in order to acquire knowledge of a specific age group. Then, through a comparison with the norm, teachers identify each student's needs. A child who may be a late bloomer and who cannot yet discriminate letters, much less remember their sounds, needs the opportunity to develop the foundational perceptual skills that children form through experience. Likewise, a child who is an early reader must have the opportunity to explore books and, if fine-motor development allows, even represent thought through writing. The environment can thus be free of the stress that results from unrealistic expectations. In this stress-free environment, children have the freedom to explore, talk, play, create, and grow according to individual timetables. Classrooms that accommodate the variances in development measure success by examining individual progress, one child at a time.

Educators must accept that the alignment of child development and early learning strategies is a complex undertaking. This complexity demands the absence of an either-or approach and the adoption of a both-and mentality. The time has come for the emergence of a model for Christian early education that respects the full breadth of what our children are ready to do and should be doing. We must place ourselves in the center of this exciting experiment and believe that God will lead us because He loves little children and does not want to see a single child fail or underachieve. God is "intimately acquainted with all [their] ways" (Psalm 139:3), and through His leadership He will direct us to a place that honors those ways. Under God's supervision we know enough to get us there. What may hold us back is a refusal to accept that we have not yet arrived. And what will result from excellence in education? The children will be emotionally healthy and academically prepared, and they will not only satisfy curriculum standards but also feel competent as learners and prepared for future academic challenges.

References

Armstrong, Thomas. 2006. *The best schools: How human development research should inform educational practice.* Alexandria, VA: Association for Supervision and Curriculum Development.

Damon, William. 1988. *The moral child: Nurturing children's natural moral growth.* New York: Free Press.

Friedman, Thomas L. 2006. *The world is flat: A brief history of the twenty-first century.* 1st rev. and exp. ed. New York: Farrar, Straus and Giroux.

Jensen, Eric. 2005. *Teaching with the brain in mind.* 2nd ed. Alexandria, VA: Association for Supervision and Curriculum Development.

Pink, Daniel H. 2005. *A whole new mind: Moving from the Information Age to the Conceptual Age.* New York: Riverhead Books.

REFLECTION

Getting from Point [A] to Point [B] Without Going Crazy! The [A][B][C]s of Curriculum Mapping

By D'Arcy Maher, Cheryl Cranston, Leanne Leak, and Milton Uecker.
Reprinted from *CEE*, November 2005.

My marriage was just a few days old when I realized that my new husband was about the *journey*—not about the *map*. We found significant cause for hilarity because every street name in Honolulu looks the same (with only 13 letters in the Hawaiian alphabet, you can see why). Quite opposite of my husband, I consider a day with an atlas time well spent ... no laughing, please.

The number one subject that generates questions for our department is curriculum. The elementary and secondary education fields have come to some consensus about what children should learn (scope) and when they should learn it (sequence) within the various grade levels. In the field of early education, a scope and sequence is just now being defined. Directors struggle to articulate one for the teachers in their program, and teachers just as eagerly want to participate in constructing the framework from which they will teach.

Are We Prepared?

In an early education center, children are about the *journey*; as educators we have the responsibility to be about the *map*. Parents depend on our education, experience, and expertise to move their children toward competence and school readiness. Are we prepared?

Curriculum Is Not ...

- Something purchased from a publisher
- A workbook series
- A packaged teacher guide of activities
- Synonymous with workbooks or teacher guides

Curriculum Is ...

- The design of experiences and activities developed by teachers to help children increase their competence; it should be thought of as everything that happens to children during their time at the early education center (Hendrick 1990, 2)

- Everything that learners experience in school (Van Brummelen 2002, 20)
- The *map* we use to guide the children's *journey*, intentionally enhancing the trip through multiple teaching strategies, with the various roads (strategies) all leading to one destination (expected student outcomes)

The Legend

Guiding statements delineate the program's foundational beliefs: statements of faith, mission, vision, and core values. Always a ready reference, these statements provide the context or foundation for developing the curriculum.

The Compass Rose

The **philosophy of teaching and learning** articulates the program beliefs about how children learn and how they should be instructed, guided, and assessed. The statement highlights the importance of the relationship between the child and the teacher and between development and maturity. It also addresses spiritual growth and development in young children. The statement determines the instructional methods and design deemed appropriate in light of the program's view of the nature and needs of children. The importance of this statement cannot be ignored, and when properly based on Scripture and research, it determines the direction of the program.

> Often [directors] give teachers [workbooks or a packaged teacher guide] alone for instructional direction, so these teachers then believe that their primary objective is to complete the books. But if [workbooks or a packaged teacher guide] determine the curriculum, publishers have made the important curricular and instructional decisions for your [early education center]. No thinking [director] wants to choose that option. (Gangel 2002, 150)

The Destination

Visualize the destination by developing an accountability document: **expected student outcomes** (ends). In clear, compelling, and descriptive language, the expected student outcomes state competencies the children will have attained when they leave the program. The age-appropriate outcomes address the spiritual, social/emotional, cognitive, and physical developmental domains and may even address the impact the program wishes to have on the parents as well.

The Route

On the basis of those outcomes, broad goals and objectives for each age group represented in the program are developed with careful intentionality, acknowledging the uneven growth of children through overlap of expectations among age groups. **Sub-outcomes** further define the plan by revealing the building blocks (or underlying components of the expected student outcomes) that help teachers target their efforts. Depending on the nature of the program, the sub-outcomes may be intentionally delivered through themes or skill emphasis. Specific **content objectives** (knowledge, skill, and disposition) provide guidance for weekly lesson plans, building on one another to achieve the monthly objectives (or sub-outcomes). The planning of the classroom environment and of the materials available for children to choose from addresses outcomes that are attained through children's ongoing, direct experiences in the class over time.

As the sub-outcomes and content objectives are carefully determined, the planning is further refined to place them according to an intentional **sequence**. All pieces logically build on one another, and the sequence actually provides a scaffold the children can use to succeed.

The Journey

Teaching strategies (means) enhance the children's journey by providing various options to employ when fully engaging the children. On the basis of an understanding of the nature and needs of children, strategies and materials for engaging the children are given, balanced schedules are developed, and guidelines for the physical/emotional environment are provided. Imagine the variety: child-initiated activities; teacher-directed instruction; exploration; sensory experiences; guided discovery; large-group, small-group, and individual choice; learning centers; indoor and outdoor environments.

Are We There Yet?

Informal assessment (outcomes) occurs naturally within the daily class schedule. The teacher collects observations, creates portfolios, and conducts interviews—all of which provide crucial information about instruction modification

for the whole class or for individual students. As children master concepts, the teacher moves ahead to the next concept, theme, or skill to be introduced.

The Benefits

The programwide curriculum map provides a platform for teacher success. Teachers know the direction of the program; they know **what** to teach, **when** to introduce concepts, **how** to implement the curriculum, and **where** they have succeeded. Teachers and their assistants easily see how their contributions move the children toward the anticipated destination of expected student outcomes.

Packing for the Journey

Some teachers think that this kind of curriculum map stifles their creativity. Think of this analogy: You're going on a trip and want to take only one small suitcase. You need to have clothing for three very different types of activities. Your creativity soars! Every piece of clothing you place in your bag must have multiple uses; every piece must "make the team." A curriculum map actually releases your creativity because each activity and experience must be intentionally planned to be meaningful for the children and assist them in reaching the predetermined goals and objectives.

As you develop the programwide curriculum map, you will discover that no *one* published resource will meet all the goals and objectives you have for the children; this fact explains why *curriculum* is not something purchased from a publisher. Most likely you will use a blend of resources to address the needs of the children and to support effective teaching strategies.

Comments for Teachers

Generally, the program director develops the programwide curriculum map. Perhaps this process does not exist in your program, or maybe your classroom is part of a school system that has an encompassing curriculum plan for the K–12 program but does not address your lone early education classroom. Individual teachers can move through this process to create and address the goals and objectives for the age group they teach.

My Adventure

My first starring role in an early education program was to guide children ages 12 to 18 months from 3:00 to 6:00 p.m. in the toddler room. "Turn in lesson plans with the activities you will do with the children," I was instructed. The large, well-respected program had not developed any guidelines or expected student outcomes. In addition, the morning teacher's lesson plans were so filled with lists of routines that I could not get a clear picture of what activities the director intended to include. And I perceived that the activities had to be large-group, teacher-directed instruction ... and I knew that wouldn't happen. During those early days, I felt as if I were herding cats!

Thankfully, my college courses provided some guidance. By reviewing age expectations and developmental checklists, I came to realize several things:

- The *routine care* components, which make up much of the daily schedule with this age group, would be the primary vehicle for packaging the activities.
- Activities would be most successful in small-group or one-on-one interactions.
- Meaningful activities would be relatively simple, providing an opportunity for the children to explore something unfamiliar with their senses.
- My desire to do cute craft projects with the children would result in activities of little or no meaning for them.
- The importance of the activities was credible when tied back to child development textbook materials and/or developmental checklists, and therefore it was easy to explain their purposes to the director and to inquiring parents.

Even as a young, bumbling teacher, I realized the need for and helpfulness of a map. My confidence grew when I established a destination for the children in the classroom.

13

Guiding Statements (Legend)

Mission, Vision, and Core Values

Philosophy of Teaching and Learning (Compass Rose)

A philosophy of teaching and learning includes perspectives on the care and education of young children—specifically, what learning *looks like* for young children, that is, how children learn, the relationship between development and maturity, and the role of assessment. This statement also addresses the process of spiritual growth and formation in young children and answers the question, What does Scripture say about ministry to young children?

Expected Student Outcomes (Destination)

What competencies will children have attained when they leave your program in the following areas of development: spiritual, social/emotional, cognitive, and physical?

Goals and Objectives for Each Age Group:	Sub-outcomes	Sequence
Content (that will be covered), **skills** (that will be introduced), and **disposition** (emerging values, beliefs, and attitudes)	Objectives that build toward the programwide expected student outcomes	• Realistic • Targeted, but flexible enough to address the uneven development of children

Scope
(Route)

Tells teachers **what** the curriculum will cover

Sequence
(Route)

Tells teachers **when** to introduce concepts

> ## Strategies (Journey)
> Create a **Learning Context** that flows from the nature/needs of the learner
>
> Tell teachers **how** to implement the curriculum

schedule *environment* *materials*

> ## Assessment (Are We There Yet?)
> **Formative (informal)**
>
> **Summative (formal)**
>
> **Assessment plan**: philosophy, methods, tools
>
> Tells teachers **where** they've succeeded

> ## Destination
> Children reflecting the expected
> student outcomes of your center

15

Conclusion

Numerous Scriptures portray a God who has a plan—a plan for humanity, a plan for the redemption of humans, and a plan for us individually. This truth gives us great comfort and security. *Planning*, if you will, is an activity of our sovereign God. When we plan, we express the character of God, and this expression promotes the confidence of our stakeholders—staff, parents, and yes, even children.

Preparations can begin **today**. As you develop and refine the *map*, you will notice that the *journey* becomes much more pleasant and productive.

References

Gangel, Kenneth O., ed. 2002. *Called to lead: Understanding and fulfilling your role as an educational leader.* Colorado Springs, CO: Purposeful Design Publications.

Hendrick, Joanne. 1990. *Total learning.* 3rd ed. Columbus, OH: Merrill Publishing.

Van Brummelen, Harro. 2002. *Steppingstones to curriculum: A biblical path.* 2nd ed. Colorado Springs, CO: Purposeful Design Publications.

REFLECTION

Rubric for Assessment of Curricular Resources for Early Education Classrooms

By Rebecca Carwile. Reprinted from *CEE*, November 2005.

Editor's Note: Choosing appropriate curricular resources can be a daunting task. The rubric on the following pages, designed for use by early educators, will assist your efforts to provide children with intentional and meaningful experiences.

Instructions

Review the text/materials carefully. Assess the material for each of the categories listed. Rate the material on the continuum as directed. The descriptor in the first column receives a rating of 1, the descriptor in the middle column receives a rating of 3, and the descriptor in the third column receives a rating of 5.

Scoring

Multiply the ranking by the prioritization factor predetermined by your curriculum team. Compute the total scaled score for the material.

Category Prioritization: Prior to using the scale, your curriculum review team and/or program faculty should rank the categories in order, with 5 the most important and 1 the least important. Number the categories from 1 to 5 in the column labeled Category Prioritization.

Category Total: The Category Total is the combined value of the rating of the elements in the Category. For example, the Category Total for Spiritual Applications is the sum of the ratings for the first two rows of the rubric.

Scaled Total: Multiply the Category Total by the Category Prioritization. That product is the Scaled Total.

When deciding on which curriculum resources to use, rate each component of the set (for example, comparing the preliteracy materials of several companies) and then compare the Scaled Totals.

Category	Weak	Adequate	Strong
Rating Scale	1	3	5

The sum of the rating scale in any given category of the rubric becomes the **Category Total** for that category on the scoring chart.

Category	Category Prioritization	x Category Total	= Scored Total
Spiritual Applications			
Curriculum Correlation			
Developmental Appropriateness			
Functionality			
Cost Effectiveness			
			Column Total:

Category	Weak	Adequate	Strong
Rating Scale	1	3	5
Spiritual Applications	The philosophy of the text/materials does not reflect Christian values.	The philosophy of the text/materials is not against Christian values.	The philosophy of the text/materials reflects strong Christian values.
	The images in the text/materials do not reflect Christian values.	The images in the text/materials are not in opposition to Christian values and could be used by the teacher to support Christian beliefs.	The images in the text/materials are designed to reflect Christian values so clearly that the children can interpret the values without teacher assistance.
Curriculum Correlation	The text/materials do not have stated objectives.	The text/materials include basic objectives that show some correlation to the program's scope and sequence.	The objectives presented for the text/materials directly correspond with the objectives in the program's scope and sequence.
	The text/materials are not designed for instruction that leads to mastery of the program's stated goals and objectives.	The text/materials can be adapted for use in instruction that leads to the mastery of the program's stated goals and objectives.	The objectives of the text/materials match the program's stated goals and objectives.

Category	Weak	Adequate	Strong
Rating Scale	**1**	**3**	**5**
Developmental Appropriateness	The developmental level of the materials is not consistent and/or is not easily identified.	The developmental levels can be determined by the teacher with careful analysis.	The developmental levels are clearly indicated, and the activities are consistent with the expectations of the indicated levels.
	The material requires children to complete paper-and-pencil tasks significantly more than it engages them in manipulative, exploratory activity.	The material provides opportunity for the teacher to blend paper and pencil activity with manipulative, exploratory activity.	The material offers children the opportunity to manipulate concrete materials and to explore concepts significantly more than it engages them in paper-and-pencil tasks.
	The text/materials do not provide recommendations for children with differing learning styles.	The text/materials could be adapted to provide for children with differing learning styles.	The text/materials provide appropriate recommendations for children with differing learning styles.
	The text/materials do not provide recommendations for children with differing learning abilities.	The text/materials could be adapted to provide for children with differing learning abilities.	The text/materials provide multiple recommendations for children with differing learning abilities.
	The text/materials do not include multicultural images and activities.	The text/materials provide multicultural images but do not offer suggestions for multicultural experiences.	The text/materials provide multicultural images and multiple suggestions for multicultural experiences.
	The text/materials do not include objectives that are aligned with professional standards.	The text/materials include objectives that are aligned with professional standards for at least two of the areas of development.	The text/materials include specific objectives for each area of development, and these are aligned with professional standards.
	The text/materials are limited to stimulation in one developmental area.	The text/materials could be used by the teacher to stimulate growth in multiple areas of development.	The text/materials have clearly defined application to each of the areas of growth and development.

19

Category	Weak	Adequate	Strong
Rating Scale	1	3	5
Functionality	The materials lack visual appeal or are outdated.	The materials are colorful and current.	The materials are visually engaging and use colors and designs that are appealing to children.
	The student materials are not packaged and are difficult for children to handle.	The materials can be managed and used by the children, and the packaging of the materials facilitates their use.	The materials are easy for children to use, and a means of organizing and storing them is provided.
	There are no teacher support materials.	The teacher support materials are generalized and offer some suggestions for implementation.	The teacher support materials are focused and provide specific suggestions or guidance for implementation.
	The teacher support materials are difficult to organize and work with.	The teacher support materials are manageable.	The teacher support materials are organized, self-contained, and easy to use.
Cost Effectiveness	The materials are intended to be consumable and must be completely replaced after one use.	The materials are intended to be reusable, and the consumable elements are presented as a reproducible master.	The materials are intended to be reusable and are not dependent on consumable elements.
	The materials will not withstand "kid wear."	The materials are strong enough to be used for a short time.	The materials are durable and can be used repeatedly over a long time.
	The materials are limited to one specific age group.	The materials can be adapted for use with more than one age group.	The materials are designed to be used by a number of age groups for multiple purposes.
	The initial cost of the materials is in excess of $25 per student.	The initial cost of the materials is between $15 and $25 dollars per student.	The initial cost is less than $15 per student.
	Teacher support materials must be purchased in addition to the student materials.	Some teacher support materials are provided with the purchase of the student materials, while others must be purchased.	All necessary teacher support materials are provided with the purchase of the student materials.

Building a Classroom Community That Values Children

By Janet Arndt. Reprinted from *CEE*, May 2006.

Every day children run the risk of facing issues that cause them to lose the innocence of childhood. Divorce, television's crisis news, fear of strangers or intruders, long hours in childcare, and economic demands made on parents force children to deal with topics once reserved for adults. Parents, schools, the media, and our culture share information with children that causes stress and anxiety. As sociologist James Garbarino (1995) describes in the title of his book, we are "raising children in a socially toxic environment." This socially toxic environment makes children grow up too fast, both socially and emotionally. For some children, teachers may be the only lifelines to a childhood.

The Challenge

The culture of America can be hostile to raising children. The media sing of junk food, name-brand clothing, and violence. Very few companies recognize the importance of family life by offering their employees flexible hours and accommodating work schedules (Olfman 2005; Samenow 1998). Consumerism is the value most often placed on children.

Recent brain research shows that lack of social-emotional support can adversely affect learning ability as well as the quality of life of young children (Greenspan 1999; Jensen 1998). A physical reaction in the brain occurs when children undergo a constant state of stress. If this stress increases and continues over time, children can develop significant problems in learning because of physiological changes in the brain (Jensen 1998). Christian teachers, uniquely placed, provide social-emotional support for young children to rise above the stress that is present today.

Wisdom from the Lord

As Christians, we value our children as gifts from God who bear His image (as do we) and for whose development we will give an account. The value of children is clear in Scripture. In the Psalms we read, "Sons are a heritage from the Lord, children a reward from him.... Blessed is the man whose quiver is full of them" (127:3–5). With God's gift comes responsibility.

In the New Testament, Jesus reiterated the value of children. "And whoever welcomes a little child like this in my name welcomes me" (Matthew 18:5). "See that you do not look down on one of these little ones. For I tell you that their angels in heaven always see the face of my Father in heaven" (Matthew 18:10). Jesus also said, "Let the little children come to me, and do not hinder them, for the kingdom of heaven belongs to such as these" (Matthew 19:14).

It is clear in Scripture how the Lord views not only children but also the responsibility that adults have regarding children. Christian teachers of young children, acting in the absence of parents during the school day and having an obligation to the Lord, need to get their guidance from these verses. The Christian culture must respond to the needs of children so that the children's importance and value is made clear to them even if the surrounding secular culture fails in this task.

Actions Speak Louder Than Words

Begin your school year by praying for each child and family: that God's strength and power will help you meet their needs despite the challenges they present. Ask God to give you a special love for every one of the children in your care as well as a sensitivity to the issues that affect their lives.

The first weeks of a new school year should focus on building a community. It is important for children to feel that they belong to a community and that they are contributing members. Children should learn one another's names, help create classroom rules, be assigned classroom jobs, and learn assertive words. These activities give children a sense of belonging and well-being as well as a voice in their world.

Learning Names

Circle time provides a daily opportunity to welcome each student by name. It is widely agreed that using songs or rhymes in this process adds to stimulation of neurons and brain growth. This activity highlights each child and also gives the other children a chance to learn the names of their classmates. Learning one another's names gives the children the tools necessary to engage their classmates in meaningful social ways.

Names give value to each person. Instead of saying, "That girl took my toy," Joni can say, "Alisha took my toy!" This personalization allows the teacher to ask Joni, "What should you say to Alisha?" The problem-solving process begins rather than the detective game that wastes precious moments.

In addition, when children know names of their classmates, they can share classroom experiences with their own families. Many times parents want to establish friendships with families who have children of the same age. Facilitating these connections for families is a good way to help support the children's social-emotional growth.

Creating Classroom Rules

When a new group of children gathers in the classroom for the first time, it is important for them to realize that your role as the teacher is not only to teach them but also to keep them safe. Since the classroom is a community of learners, rules to live by must be formed so that all the children understand the expectations for behavior. The children should help develop a list of behaviors recognized as important for a respectful community. Using the brainstorming method, whereby the children share their ideas as the teacher writes the ideas on the board, gives all the children a voice in the process. Sometimes the children generate ideas, and other times they cannot think of anything. The teacher either guides the process by making suggestions on grouping the same ideas under a different word or leads the children in thinking about ideas that are important to classroom management. The product should be a culmination of their ideas—a culmination that is simply put and easy to understand. The classroom rules should be written on a large poster for all to see. Using a picture next to the rule will help those who are not yet reading. For example, the poster might picture two hands next to "Take turns" and two feet next to "Walk in the classroom." Reviewing the rules during circle time the first few weeks of school helps the students feel the importance of their work. Often the children remind their friends when the rules are not being followed.

Assigning Classroom Jobs

Children learn to be responsible by having responsibility. Classroom jobs are a wonderful way to teach this skill. The jobs should change daily so that all the children have a job every few days. This rotation keeps the idea of a job fresh and less burdensome. In addition to the importance of having formal jobs, children need to learn to put away materials after they have played or finished using them. Holding the children accountable for their actions teaches them responsibility. Sometimes, as teachers, we can easily conclude that it is quicker and easier to do a task alone. That may be! However, the teachable moments are lost when we do things for children that they can do for themselves. In addition, the message we are conveying to the child is "I don't think you can do it the way I want it done."

If we want to help develop competent children, they need opportunities to demonstrate competence. Requiring that they follow through on their responsibility is a gift you give to them. Remember Proverbs 22:6: "Train a child in the way he should go, and when he is old he will not turn from it." This admonition applies to physical actions in addition to the spiritual realm.

Learning Assertive Words

Children need to have the words to stand up for themselves so that they do not resort to physical means to handle disputes. Teachers may tell children they should take turns. However, when taking turns goes awry, children need the words to state their issue. Many times teachers say to the child, "Use your words!" but children may not know the words to use. Teaching children simple statements such as "I don't like it when you take an extra turn" or "I don't want you to take my ball—please stop!" is helpful.

When we teach children to use assertive language, we empower them to take action. Develop a strategy whereby children will ask an adult to help after trying three times to solve the problem on their own. If it is a dangerous situation, they should be told to get an adult immediately. With a plan in place, children are able to act appropriately in their own defense.

And Finally

Christian teachers have the God-given job of helping children successfully navigate through their environment and the challenges it presents. When teachers help children develop their social-emotional well-being and teach them strategies to be successful, children will develop the resilience needed to stand strong.

References

Garbarino, J. 1995. *Raising children in a socially toxic environment*. San Francisco, CA: Jossey-Bass.

Greenspan, S. 1999. *Building healthy minds: The six experiences that create intelligence and emotional growth in babies and young children*. With N. B. Lewis. New York: Perseus Books.

Jensen, E. 1998. *Teaching with the brain in mind*. Alexandria, VA: Association for Supervision and Curriculum Development.

Olfman, S., ed. 2005. *Childhood lost: How American culture is failing our kids*. Westport, CT: Praeger Publishers.

Samenow, S. 1998. *Before it's too late: Why some kids get into trouble—and what parents can do about it*. Rev. ed. New York: Times Books.

Additional Reading

Barker, K., ed. 1995. *The NIV study Bible*. Grand Rapids, MI: Zondervan.

Bergen, D., and J. Coscia. 2001. *Brain research and childhood education: Implications for educators*. Olney, MD: Association for Childhood Education International.

Hulbert, A. 2003. *Raising America: Experts, parents, and a century of advice about children*. New York: Alfred A. Knopf.

Zelizer, V. A. 1985. *Pricing the priceless child*. New York: Basic Books.

REFLECTION

Section 1 Authors

Janet S. Arndt, EdD, celebrates children in her role as an assistant professor of education in early childhood at Gordon College in Wenham, Massachusetts. She and her husband, Kenneth, have four children—all of whom attended a Christian school over an hour's drive from their home.

Rebecca F. Carwile, EdD, was an education professor at Liberty University in Lynchburg, Virginia. She spoke frequently at ACSI conferences and conventions. Rebecca was the first recipient of ACSI's Early Education Lifetime Achievement Award before her death on January 6, 2006.

Cheryl Cranston is an inspirational speaker, an educational trainer, and a health coach. With over 27 years of experience in the field of education, she holds a master's degree in education and a bachelor's degree in speech communication. Currently, she serves as adjunct faculty in the Child Development Program at Vanguard University, while also guest speaking at various conferences and events around the country. Cheryl is known for her humor and her ability to educate, motivate, and inspire—helping early educators look "through the eyes of a child."

Leanne Leak, BA, serves as ACSI's western states early education field director. Leanne is conversant in early education policy and accreditation, and she maintains her knowledge base in early education through continual reading, synthesis, and study. She is in the process of completing a graduate degree.

D'Arcy Maher, MEd, serves as ACSI's director of Early Education Services. She is also the managing editor of *Christian Early Education* magazine.

Milton Uecker, EdD, is academic dean of the Graduate School at Columbia International University in Columbia, South Carolina. He has served in educational programs for more than 40 years as a teacher and an administrator in schools in Korea, Texas, and Virginia. He earned his doctorate with an emphasis in early childhood education.

Section 2: Assessment

Assessment: The Key to Arriving at Your Destination

By Shannon Chambley. Reprinted from *CEE*, March 2006.

Quality early childhood programs have curricula in place that include clearly stated, well-defined, developmentally appropriate learning outcomes. These curricula provide a road map of where you want children to go. But knowing where you want to go and what you want children to achieve is only the itinerary for your trip. You must evaluate your progress along the way to see whether you are still on course.

You can use many strategies to effectively assess children, but the first and most important step is to plan for assessment. When you are planning the lessons you will teach, you must also plan your assessment. Examine your lesson plans carefully. What skills are you presenting, and how will you assess both the effectiveness of your instruction and the growth of individual children? Assessment will not happen effectively if you do not plan for it to take place. The most effective assessment of young children has multiple layers and seeks to observe children in a variety of activities and in a variety of ways. Portfolios can provide this multilayered approach to assessment. But what is a portfolio, and how do you manage this type of assessment in a busy preschool classroom?

Portfolios

A portfolio is a very effective way to track and measure the progress of a child. Beginning a portfolio for a child can be as simple as labeling a file folder with the child's name. The folder can then be filled with items such as skill checklists, anecdotal notes, samples of the child's work, and pictures of tasks that the child has performed. Not only does a well-maintained portfolio help you track the progress of individual students, but it can also be an excellent tool for conveying that progress to parents. A comprehensive portfolio presented during a parent conference can help parents literally see the progress their child has made. It can also help build a bridge between school and home by demonstrating to parents that you fully understand their child's development and progress. All children will experience growth in some area, even if they are not experiencing success in all areas. Especially when children demonstrate this type of growth, a portfolio can help communicate to parents that you have an appreciation for the whole child. Finally, a portfolio can also serve as an end-of-the-year gift, providing parents with a sort of preschool scrapbook.

Skill Checklists

Your assessment plan may include a developmental checklist of skills that you are teaching in a given week, month, or school year. The checklist should include opportunities to observe a skill more than once. You need to record skill progression in such a way that you are showing respect for the individuality of children by using codes or terms such as mastery (M), progressing (P), or not yet (NY). For each observation, it is very important to note the date you made it. For a sample checklist go to www.acsi.org/~eeresources.

Anecdotal Notes

An anecdotal note is a brief written description of an observed behavior. As you interact with the children, you have countless opportunities to make observations. These observations are valuable because they can reveal patterns of behavior and progress or can reveal delays in skill development. You can also use analyses of these observations to construct future lesson plans that meet the needs of the children. Observing children may be easy, but recording observations can be difficult in an active early childhood classroom. You can date and record observations on sticky notes and place them in the portfolios. Another option is to print self-adhesive mailing labels with "Name," "Date," and codes for the type of skill and for the time you observed it. Skill codes might include L for language/literacy, M for math, SS for social skills, and FM for fine-motor skills. Codes for the time you made the observation might include C for centers, CT for circle time, and SG for small group. You can record several notes on one sheet of labels and then peel the labels off and place them in individual portfolios at a later time. Before the observations, you can put the name of each child on a label to ensure that you record observations on all the children. Another way to make sure you observe all the children is to set up a calendar or a schedule for daily observations or to plan to observe all the children as they rotate through a given center or activity.

Work Samples and Photographs

Work samples are also an excellent way to track the children's progress. Collecting and assessing the work of the children gives you insight into their development and also provides supporting documentation for checklists. After observing a child painting at the easel, you can ask the child's permission to keep the painting in a special place until the end of the year. Then you can record on the back what you observed during the painting process. For example, you might write, "Free-floating 'big head' figure has emerged including strokes of color that appear to be legs, 8/25/05." As this child continues to progress in painting, the figure will appear grounded, and arms, legs, and other body parts will be clear. A collection of this child's work with anecdotal notes and dates can clearly demonstrate the progress the child is making in developing fine-motor and emergent literacy skills. If children decide they cannot part with a painting or a drawing, make a photocopy. Work samples should include both child-initiated, spontaneous work and work that children produce in response to your request. During parent conferences, you will experience another benefit of collecting work samples because you will be able to pull out a sample of a child's work and share with parents what it tells you about their child's development. Not only do these work samples communicate your understanding of the child, but they can also help educate parents about the value of play and of quality preschool experiences. **Including photographs in a portfolio is way of collecting work samples that may not fit into a portfolio.** Photos might include pictures of a block structure that a child created, a pattern that a child reproduced and continued with manipulatives, or a child walking on a balance beam.

You have observed behaviors and skill development and have marked them on your checklist. You have recorded factual anecdotal notes and have collected samples of work. What are you going to do with the information? You need to take the information you have gained since you started out on this trip, and plot your progress toward your destination. You must seek to ensure that your lesson plans not only reflect the abilities and the individualities of the children in your class but also provide opportunities for scaffolding future learning experiences. You will never arrive at the place you want to be if you don't check your map and make sure you're heading in the right direction.

A Final Note ...

As many states implement or make plans for universal prekindergarten programs, there is much attention being paid to preschool screenings/assessments that consist of pretests and posttests. While these tools may provide accurate information about a child on a given day, early educators should view them as only one piece of a comprehensive assessment plan and not the plan itself.

REFLECTION

Observation: More Than Meets the **E**ye ...

By Stacia Emerson. Reprinted from *CEE*, March 2006.

Remember when you were in elementary school and you thought your teacher had eyes in the back of her head because she knew everything that happened in the classroom? Well, if that's the case, just think about early childhood teachers! They need to have keen eyesight and the ability to observe from all angles in order to assess children's development and progress effectively.

Observation is a very valuable tool for assessing children of all ages. **Teachers and caregivers can learn most observation techniques quickly,** and the techniques will work in assessing *all* developmental learning areas. Two widely used observation methods are anecdotal records and running records.

Anecdotal Records

- These are brief descriptions of a *certain* behavior that is of interest to the observer.
- These factual accounts of behavior do not contain subjective, judgmental language such as "uncooperative" or "in a bad mood." The observer can include these comments parenthetically or separately.
- These records include the date, time, and setting of the behavior.
- The observer does not require any special training to complete these records.
- The observer usually creates these records after, not while, the behavior occurs.

(Beaty 2005; Wortham 2001)

Running Records

- The observer writes these detailed descriptions of a child's behavior as it occurs.
- The observer writes down everything that happens while observing a particular child.

33

- The language in these records is brief and abbreviated so that the observer can record behavior quickly while it is happening.
- The observer should record only the facts.
- These records provide a lot of information about a child because the observer writes down everything that is happening, not just specified behaviors.

(Beaty 2005; Wortham 2001)

You can use both of these observation techniques on various age-groups. When implementing these techniques, consider the following:

Infants

- Remember that the goal of observing infants should be to document developmental milestones and assess general health.
- Locate a comprehensive, reliable developmental checklist so that milestones can be dated and checked when they have been reached.
- Keep sticky notepads and index cards around the center so that you can record behavior quickly and easily. You can keep these notes in the child's folder, and you can transfer the information to a checklist as appropriate.
- Observe infants on a regular basis. They change so quickly that it is necessary to note changes weekly and biweekly.
- Communicate the information to parents as needed. You need to give some information daily (food intake, diaper changes, sleep patterns). You can give other information during scheduled conferences.

Toddlers

- Continue to use observation to determine developmental milestones. Toddlers will all go through the same stages of development and in the same order, but at different rates. Observe toddlers as individuals.
- Consider information from any observation private, and do not share it with others without the parent's permission.
- Because toddlers cannot express themselves fully through language, observing their daily activities is one of the most accurate ways to assess them (Wortham 2001).

- Observe toddlers in a systematic, organized way that will give the whole picture of the toddler's day. Keeping a chart of observations will help ensure that you have made observations for each child and during different activities of the day.
- Observation is especially helpful in documenting toddlers' progress in social development since two- and three-year-olds are just beginning to become part of a group.

Preschoolers

- Anecdotal records can provide cumulative information. If you use them over time, you can ascertain valuable details about children (Beaty 2005). You can include this information to help create a portfolio, to back up information from a checklist, and to plan appropriately for children, especially if they require intervention.
- Observing preschoolers during their self-selected center time can give you necessary information to plan appropriately for their future center experiences.
- When writing down the information, record only the facts (do not interpret), and keep them in chronological order (Beaty 2005).
- Use descriptive words but not judgmental words (Beaty 2005).

- You need to be familiar with child development and with the goals of the program to be able to transfer the information about the behavior of children to information you can use for understanding their developmental level and for planning (Wortham 2001).
- Remember that the presence of an observer can influence the behavior of children and thus can make the information unreliable. Be as unobtrusive as possible by following these tips:
  - Sit near the children but do not interact with them.
  - Dress in a way that does not stand out.
  - Wait a few minutes until the children get used to being observed before you record information (Wortham 2001).

35

References
Beaty, Janice J. 2005. *Observing development of the young child.* 6th ed. Upper Saddle River, NJ: Prentice Hall.
Wortham, Sue C. 2001. *Assessment in early childhood education.* 4th ed. Upper Saddle River, NJ: Prentice Hall.

REFLECTION

More Than a Test: Constructing a True Picture from Multiple Sources

By D'Arcy Maher. Reprinted from *CEE*, March 2006.

A few years back, I had to take the GRE (Graduate Record Exam) for entrance into graduate school. I prepared (using one of the many popular GRE study helps), went to bed early the night before, ate a healthy breakfast the morning of the test (sans my typical breakfast beverage of Coke), and arrived at the testing center early. In spite of my preparation, I still had sweaty palms and felt as though I couldn't keep a thought in my head.

As I drove away from the testing center, I thought, "I am more than that test. How can a computer know my attitude of determination or my relationship with others? It is crazy to put so much emphasis on a test." Three of my close friends had a similar experience with the test! Even though I know, as an adult, that I am more than a test, there exists a tension in the field of education to put a number or a rating on a person or a skill in order to quantify knowledge.

Outcomes delineated by legislatures and states put pressure on early education programs to use assessments that will provide stakeholders with information on the progress of children. Because young children cannot read, write, or use language to communicate effectively, early educators face a conundrum when determining the best way to collect and report accurate information.

There is a raging debate about the kind of tools to use, which are most reliable and valid, and which provide the most helpful information. There are two broad categories of assessment: formal and informal. **Formal assessment** includes those instruments that have been standardized, including the instructions, the testing environment, and the interpretation of results. **Informal assessment** refers to techniques and strategies that are ongoing, performed in the classroom, and may be either formative or summative in nature. **Formative evaluation** determines how students are progressing toward mastery of objectives. Examples of formative evaluation include checklists, rubrics, rating scales, and portfolio samples. **Summative evaluation** is a final assessment of what children have learned.

37

Examples of summative evaluation include some standardized instruments or even a completed portfolio (Wortham 2005, 89).

The process of assessment, correctly implemented, is intertwined with the teaching and learning processes. Assessment holds teachers accountable to teach, and children accountable to learn. It is the *teaching* and *learning* processes that engage educators in discussion. The components of those processes determine the choice of assessment tools and strategies.

Review these definitions, and consider their implications (Wortham 2005, 243):

- **Authentic achievement**—learning that is real and meaningful; achievement that is worthwhile
- **Authentic assessment**—an assessment that uses some type of performance by a child to demonstrate understanding
- **Authentic measure**—a measure that uses authentic assessments that include performance and application of knowledge

Three key words summarize these definitions: *meaningful*, *performance*, and *application*. In a nutshell, those three words describe the essence of what early education is about: classroom experiences should be deeply meaningful to children; children should be involved in *constructing* knowledge or *engaging* in activities, that is, in performing; and the experiences should have real meaning to their young lives—they should be able to apply, or use, the learning. Using those same words to define a successful outcome is apropos. Here we see that observation is a key to successfully assessing young children; it is directly linked. How often is this important topic discussed at your center? What additional items would you place on this list?

Advantages of Informal Assessment

1. The children have little stress.
2. The children produce knowledge.
3. Teachers can create checklists to support the outcomes of their lesson plan.
4. Teachers observe higher-order thinking in action.

Disadvantages of Informal Assessment

1. Observer bias exists.
2. Children may not construct what the teacher hoped to observe. For example, the teacher might look for expressive language and instead might see cognitive development.
3. The assessment may not tie to the program's expected student outcomes.
4. It is difficult to attach a grade or a number to the observation.

The National Early Childhood Assessment Resource Group established the following principles concerning assessment of young children (Wortham 2005, 23):

1. **"Assessment should bring about benefits for children."** Formal assessment is costly, and informal assessment can be time intensive. Do children realize the benefit of this investment either in direct services or in improved quality of the educational program in which they are enrolled? Keeping this principle in the forefront of our plan reminds us of the most important stakeholder: the child.

2. **"Assessment should be tailored to a specific purpose and should be reliable, valid, and fair for that purpose."** Misusing testing materials can lead to the collection of inaccurate information. Acting on inaccurate information can actually harm the child.

3. **"Assessment policies should be designed recognizing that reliability and validity of assessments increase with children's age."** Amen! Capturing accurate information about a young child's progress may best occur in informal situations.

4. **"Assessments should be age appropriate in both content and the method of data collection."** This principle points to the connection between curriculum planning and assessment. Without a doubt, what we teach children should be appropriate to what we know about their cognitive development—what they can know and do, and what experiences will scaffold them to the next level. Knowing that children do not perform well in unfamiliar surroundings or with abstractions should guide us in choosing methods that will provide authentic performance information.

5. **"Assessments should be linguistically appropriate, recognizing that to some extent all assessments are measures of language."** Consider the following: proficiency in English, receptive and expressive language proficiency, and latent language development within the home. What meaning will you attach to assessments if there is a delay in language acquisition or expression?

6. **"Parents should be a valued source of assessment information, as well as an audience for assessment results."** Parents can participate in ongoing assessment strategies that further involve them in their child's education.

The legislative emphasis on early education indicates that some stakeholders prefer the standardized results and that some form of standardized testing may be required of young children. Choosing the most appropriate tool to support your expected student outcomes is a significant task. We have included a rubric in this magazine to assist you with the challenge.

Assessment should be more than just a snapshot in time of a child's abilities. Assessment should provide a comprehensive picture of the uniqueness of a child. Quality observations help us collect the necessary information to create that comprehensive picture. Children are more than a test, more than a single observation—just like you, and just like me.

Additional Reading
Assessment in Early Childhood Education by Sue Wortham
Six Simple Ways to Assess Young Children by Sue Y. Gober
The Ounce Scale and *The Work Sampling System* from Pearson Early Learning
ACSI Early Education Expected Student Outcomes

REFLECTION

Review of [A]ssessment Materials

By Rebecca Carwile. Reprinted from *CEE*, March 2006.

Editor's Note: Choosing appropriate observation and assessment resources can be a daunting task. This rubric, designed for use by early educators, will assist you in your efforts to provide children with authentic formal and informal observation and assessment.

Instructions

Category Prioritization: Prior to using the scale, your assessment review team and/or program faculty should rank the categories in order, using 14 as the rank for the category believed to be most important and 1 for the category believed to be the least important of the set. Number the categories from 1 to 14 in the column labeled Category Prioritization.

Category Total: Review the materials carefully. Assess the materials according to each area listed in the Rubric (the first area being Clarity of Purpose). Rate the materials using the continuum in the Rubric. The descriptor in the first column receives a value of 0 if it is an unacceptable choice, and so on across the columns.

Scaled Total: Multiply the Category Prioritization by the Category Total to get the Scaled Total.

Column Total: Add the column of numbers under the heading Scaled Total. This number is the overall rating of the material. When deciding which assessment/test to use, compare the Column Totals.

Scoring Chart

Category	Category Prioritization	Category Total	Scaled Total
Clarity of Purpose			
Reliability			
Validity			
Manual Availability/Usability			
Revisions			
Organization			
Reporting			
Description of Score Use			
Materials Use			
Protocol Directions			
Cost			
Time for Administration			
Administrator Training			
Correlation with ACSI's Expected Student Outcomes			
Perceived Applicability			
		Column Total:	

	0 Unacceptable	1 Minimal	2 Acceptable	3 Target
Clarity of Purpose	The test does not include a description of its purpose.	The test includes a statement of purpose, but it's sketchy or vague.	The test includes a clear statement of purpose.	The test includes a clear statement of purpose and an explanation of intention.
Reliability	No reliability studies are reported.	The reliability description is generalized and not conclusive.	The reliability description is generalized, but it is conclusive.	The reliability description is specific and significant at an appropriate statistical level.
Validity	No validity studies are reported.	The validity description is generalized and not conclusive.	The validity description is generalized, but it is conclusive.	The validity description is specific and significant at an appropriate statistical level.
Manual Availability/Usability	There is no manual provided.	The directions provided are basic but somewhat sketchy.	There is a manual provided that includes directions for use and scoring, and the test is easy to use by those who have minimal experience with formal assessment.	There is a manual that provides directions for use and scoring, as well as an explanation of the test's construction. The test is easy to use by those who have minimal experience with formal assessment.
Revisions	The test has never been revised.	The test has been revised at least once in the past 20 years.	The test is systematically revised in 10-to-20-year cycles.	The test is systematically revised in cycles less than 10 years in length.

43

	0 Unacceptable	1 Minimal	2 Acceptable	3 Target
Organization	The test materials are not organized.	The test materials are somewhat organized.	The test materials are sufficiently organized to be usable.	The test materials are well organized, coded, and easy to identify.
Reporting	No reporting forms are included.	There are only scoring forms.	There are scoring forms and records for student files.	There are scoring forms, records for student files, and parent report forms.
Description of Score Use	There is no description of how scores should be used.	There is a vague, generalized description of how scores should be used.	There are explicit descriptions of how scores should be used.	There are explicit descriptions of how scores should be used, as well as statements of disclaimer.
Materials Use	The materials are difficult to understand.	The materials are vaguely understandable.	The use of the materials is explained well enough for general application.	The use of the materials is clearly explained, and there are specific directions for application.
Protocol Directions	There are no directions in each section.	There are generalized directions in each section.	There are specific directions in each section.	In each section, there are clearly articulated, specific directions that minimize user error.
Cost	The cost for each pupil is prohibitive.	The cost for each pupil would limit the number of tests administered each year.	The cost for each pupil is manageable within a school's budget.	The quality of information obtained justifies the cost for each pupil; the school should budget for the assessment.

	0 Unacceptable	1 Minimal	2 Acceptable	3 Target
Time for Administration	No descriptions of time elements are provided.	A specific time length is to be applied to all levels.	For each level of the test, time lengths are described.	For each level of the test, time lengths, as well as descriptions of time ranges for variant maturity levels, are described.
Administrator Training	Company-specific training is required for effective implementation and is offered only to those with a graduate degree.	Company-specific training is required for effective implementation and is offered to those with an undergraduate (AA, BA, or BS) degree.	Company-specific training is needed for effective implementation and is available, but no degree is needed by those who implement the test.	No formal training is required for effective implementation.
Correlation with ACSI's Expected Student Outcomes	The test does not correlate with any area of the outcomes.	The test correlates with at least one area of the outcomes.	The test correlates with several areas listed in the outcomes.	The test correlates exactly with the outcomes.
Perceived Applicability	The test is not applicable to our school's program.	The test is somewhat applicable to our school's program.	The test is applicable to our school's program.	The test is very applicable to our school's program; it is a wise use of resources.

Section 2 Authors

Rebecca F. Carwile, EdD, was an education professor at Liberty University in Lynchburg, Virginia. She spoke frequently at ACSI conferences and conventions. Rebecca was the first recipient of ACSI's Early Education Lifetime Achievement Award before her death on January 6, 2006.

Shannon Chambley is the director of First Years Preschool and Kindergarten in Oviedo, Florida. She and her husband, Mike, have three children that keep them extremely busy. If there is any free time left, she enjoys reading, running, and women's ministry.

Stacia Emerson, PhD, has served in multiple roles within early education: a teacher, a Sunday school teacher, and a college professor. She is currently a professor at Texas Wesleyan University.

D'Arcy Maher, MEd, serves as ACSI's director of Early Education Services. She is also the managing editor of *Christian Early Education* magazine.

Section 3:
Lesson Planning

Hidden Skills: Do You Have Them?

By D'Arcy Maher. Reprinted from *CEE*, August 2007.

Teaching is both science and art. While formal education is critical, part of teaching is nuanced by a calling and gifting from God. Working with young children is more than a job; it is a ministry that flows from a heart submitted to God. Out of that giftedness flow qualities that come together to create a successful teacher.

Lesson Plan Components

Knowledge and skill complement the ministry of an early educator. Specific areas of expertise strengthen the teacher's effectiveness and add meaning to the daily lives of the children. Knowledgeable lesson planning and skillful implementation of the plan provide a platform for meeting the needs of children. Isn't that the goal of an early education classroom: to meet the needs of children?

Lesson plans

- are tied to the program's goals and objectives for the age of the children in the class;
- are content rich (in all developmental domains, including the spiritual domain);
- address large-group, small-group, and individual-choice opportunities;
- include transition activities;
- reflect information gathered from observing children;
- include an assessment component;
- are adaptable to meet the individual needs of children.

However, even if every daily plan included those components, your plan still might fall flat. What *ensures* that a well-written plan will truly engage the children and meet their needs? Ah, friend, great question—thanks for asking!

49

Hidden Skill #1: Communication

Whenever I travel outside the United States, I become easily frustrated with the language barrier. On a recent trip to Budapest, Hungary, I traveled with Pat Baer, a preschool director from northern California. We arrived on Friday evening and had an all-day training for early education teachers on Saturday. We arrived at the training site, immediately feeling at home in the excitement, and took a tour of the facility with the other attendees. Just as conference attendees would do in the United States, the teachers exclaimed over classroom arrangements and wrote down ideas for displays. Early in the day, Pat turned to me and said, "I hate the Tower of Babel." I knew exactly what she meant. We were in the middle of an amazing experience and could not speak directly to any of the Hungarians! Anna and Lazslo were wonderful interpreters, but we wanted to speak directly with our colleagues. We could hear their words, but we did not understand any of them.

So it is with young children. Young children speak a specific language. Effective communication takes place when you speak *their* language, not just the language that is most comfortable for you.

I appreciate the word picture that Scripture offers about God's solution to another language barrier. In order to "speak our language," Christ put on flesh and lived among us (Philippians 2:5–8). Putting on flesh set Him in a unique position to *feel* our emotions and experience our temptations (Hebrews 4:14–16). These Scriptures give us great confidence that we are heard; we feel understood. We *hear* because we *understand* the language.

What is the language of young children?

A. Connectivity

Young children intuitively identify with someone who has genuine interest in them. You can express nonverbal interest through eye contact, a touch on the shoulder, patience while children use their words or respond to a request, and "unhurriedness." When you are using verbal expressions of interest, you remember to use a respectful tone, simple words that children can easily understand, and voice inflection that reflects excitement or enthusiasm, offers encouragement, and always honors the children—all delivered at eye level with them.

How do you write connectivity into your lesson plan? Review the pace of the day. For each activity, have you built in time that allows for unhurried exploration and plenty of conversation, or must the children hurry from one activity to another? Look carefully at the times of the day that may have a lag, for example, arrival time, departure time, and snack time. How can you redeem those times with opportunities for connection?

B. Sensitivity

In this context, the word *sensitive* implies responsiveness to the needs of children, a responsiveness that is based on our knowledge of their developmental strands. For instance, we know that children struggle with the differentiation between fact and fantasy. That small piece of knowledge informs the way we read stories, support dictation of their stories, and portray Bible stories. We also know that young children receive knowledge through their senses: what they see, hear, touch, taste, and smell. Understanding sensory engagement suggests teaching strategies that introduce concepts in a way that children can experience them.

Sensitive communication reminds the teacher that children see the world differently than adults do. Children are not small adults! They are unique in their development and maturation.

Exactly how do you portray sensitivity in lesson plans? Review the characteristics of the ages of the children in your classroom. How do you let that knowledge inform your classroom practices, from the structure of the day to the choice of activities? Are you intentional about appropriate planning?

C. Activity

Having the opportunity to spend time with my young friend Mark always leaves me with the best stories. Mark's verbal abilities are off the charts. His vocabulary surprises me. When he was three, he described his flight from India to the United States by including the name of the airline: Lufthansa. He pronounced it correctly, and often. Yet in his need for activity, Mark is a typically developing child. From the moment he steps in the door until he leaves, he is asking and doing. If there's a pause, he prods for something to do or play. And Mark is no different from the children in your classroom.

You can easily include activity in a lesson plan. You might call it *center time* or *read aloud* or *circle time*. But ... do your activities match the developmental level of the children? Do you choose activities that are meaningful and beneficial to the children? In other words, your activities may be cute or fun, but they may not have a learning outcome for the children. How do you evaluate which activities to include?

Hidden Skill #2: Imagination

A teacher expects young children to learn concepts that she has known for years. Example: the alphabet. The teacher has known the letters and sounds for years. Years. The same holds true for numbers and counting. It is energizing to learn something new, to have a new experience or adventure. How does the early education teacher remain energized when the concepts seem old or boring?

Excitement about a concept or topic transfers to the children. When I was a single teacher, I had the opportunity to travel widely. I would bring to the class some photos, postcards, small souvenirs, and a story or two about the journey. I could talk about what I saw and bring a little of the experience into the fabric of our classroom.

Interestingly, children would ask for a book about something I mentioned. Take for instance my first trip to Mississippi. I went with friends to celebrate the birthday of a family member. The family party was at a state park near the Gulf Coast. As we explored some of the trails, we came upon a three- or four-foot alligator on the path. As I told this story to my class in Washington State, they became quite interested. Alligators don't appreciate Washington's cool climate, and the children had never seen one outside the zoo. This interest in alligators became an opportunity to expand our classroom library, enrich the science center, reinforce some of the letters and sounds we learned, add vocabulary to our word box, and expand our puppet collection. I felt energized by both the children's interest and the additional concepts I was able to address on the basis of the children's interest.

Imagination isn't just about daydreaming, brainstorming, or playing. Imagination fuels creativity. Imagination sees a different way to meet a challenge, and that vision becomes so real it compels the teacher to create change. "A highly imaginative person finds new ways to do old things. With imagination, it's possible to go down the same road many times but never go down the same road twice" (Abbott).

How can you represent imagination in your lesson plans? What are *you*, the teacher, excited about? How do your interests provide a platform to engage the children? Is there a part of the day that you dread? If so, how can your imagination bring life to something that seems old or boring?

Lifelong Learning

I have the privilege and opportunity to visit quality programs around the country. I enjoy reviewing a center's brochure to learn more about the program. Very often, a program strives to introduce children to a learning environment in order for them to become lifelong learners. I consider this a worthy goal. But can we teach where we first have not ventured ourselves? Are you as a teacher still learning and growing? Are you still fascinated by adventure and life? How is your curiosity pushing you to learn something new?

Lesson planning becomes a place to capture more than a schedule of routines. It becomes a sacred plan to deepen communication with children, celebrate imagination, and express your interests as a teacher. Lesson planning allows you to express your ministry to children, a giftedness that flows out of your calling.

53

Reference
Abbott, Edward. Adventure. Poepauv. http://www.poepauv.com/books/imagination/Adventure.html.

REFLECTION

REFLECTION

Lesson Plan [E]valuation

By D'Arcy Maher. Reprinted from *CEE*, August 2007.

This tool was created for use with the article "Hidden Skills: Do You Have Them?" [on page 49].

Directions

Choose a weekly plan from your plan book. Answer these questions to determine the thoroughness of your plan.

General

Yes No

☐	☐	1.	You tied the plan to the program's goals and objectives for the age of the children in your class.
☐	☐	2.	The plan addresses all developmental domains, including the spiritual domain.
☐	☐	3.	The plan includes large-group, small-group, and individual-choice opportunities.
☐	☐	4.	The plan includes transition activities.
☐	☐	5.	The plan reflects information gathered from observing children.
☐	☐	6.	The plan includes an assessment component.
☐	☐	7.	There is evidence that you adapted the plan on the basis of the individual needs of the children.

Connectivity

Yes No

☐	☐	8.	For each activity, you have built in time that will allow for unhurried exploration and plenty of conversation.
☐	☐	9.	Arrival time, departure time, and snack time include suggestions for redeeming those routines with opportunities for connection.

55

Sensitivity

Yes No

☐ ☐ 10. Classroom practices reflect the child development principles of attention span, play, and engagement.

☐ ☐ 11. You handle routines, as much as possible, in a friendly, homelike manner rather than in an institutional manner.

Activity

Yes No

☐ ☐ 12. Activities match the developmental level of the children.

☐ ☐ 13. You choose activities that are meaningful and beneficial to the children.

☐ ☐ 14. You evaluate activities on the basis of the interest and engagement of the children, and you modify the activities to address the children's needs.

Count the number of yes statements, and refer to the scale below.

Scale

14: You're a master teacher, and you should write an article for this magazine!

10–13: You feel comfortable in your ministry. Don't get too comfortable with your level of competence! Keep growing and learning. Support the inexperienced teacher by giving encouragement and sharing ideas.

5–9: You have an opportunity to grow. Recommit to intentional lesson planning. Ask questions, observe a master teacher in action, or ask another staff member to help you evaluate your planning process. You can do it!

1–4: Whether you're new in the field or you've been serving awhile, lesson planning can be a tough skill to learn. Read all the articles in this magazine, and discuss ideas with others on your team. Don't forget the strength that comes from prayer. The Holy Spirit will give you creative ideas and energies for this task.

REFLECTION

Section 3 Author

D'Arcy Maher, MEd, serves as ACSI's director of Early Education Services. She is also the managing editor of *Christian Early Education* magazine.

Section 4:
Learning Centers and
Curricular Topics

A Child's Eye View of the Early Education Classroom

Compiled by Leanne Leak. Reprinted from *CEE*, November 2007.

Whether their workplace is called a preschool, an early learning center, a prekindergarten, or a child development program, early educators all share a desire to spark learning and growth in the children in their classroom. One of the best ways to do so is to establish well-defined centers that help children select activities and engage in learning. Effective learning centers include ample materials that are attractively arranged to invite children's participation, and these centers are separated from other areas in the classroom so that children can sink deeply into an activity.

The View from Above

If a tiny airplane flew through the window and snapped an aerial photograph of your classroom, what would the picture reveal? Clearly defined play areas where small groups of children choose from interesting activities? A runway or large open space in the center of the room? Perhaps your classroom lies somewhere between those two extremes.

Successful classrooms have clearly defined areas of interest and activity, and the children access these areas through clear pathways. The interest centers do not need to be large spaces, or even permanent ones, as you may modify them from week to week to reflect changing curriculum themes. **An effective interest center is simply an organized, defined space that encourages children to engage in autonomous learning.** The space must be flexible enough to accommodate all the day's activities. For instance, the carpeted block-building area can serve as the area for circle times.

The following guidelines will help you plan classroom space:

- Place calm, quiet areas away from active, noisy areas to minimize distractions and potential disruptions to play and learning.
- Because materials that are close together will inevitably be used together, arrange compatible activities near one another, particularly when they share resources such as a sink.

61

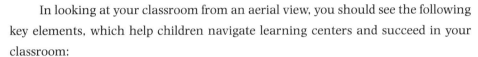

- Provide space that is varied and appropriately sized to meet the needs of the specific activity, providing some play spaces designed for just one or two children and others for as many as four to six children.

- Have a sufficient *number* of activities available so that the children have plenty to choose from when they complete an activity. It is recommended that free-choice time provide from 1 1/2 to 2 1/2 more activities than the number of children who will be playing. This ratio minimizes overcrowding and ensures enough variety to capture children's interest (Kritchevsky, Prescott, and Walling 1977).

In looking at your classroom from an aerial view, you should see the following key elements, which help children navigate learning centers and succeed in your classroom:

Boundaries

Interest areas need clear boundaries, with physical markers separating them. A bookshelf or a storage unit may provide a boundary, stabilized by sufficient width at the base so that it cannot be easily tipped over. Small free-standing room dividers can also provide a visual separation between play spaces. At four feet, they are high enough to block the children's view of other areas but low enough to allow adults to see over them. A space can also be defined by something as simple as an area rug, a tape line on the floor, or a change in flooring from linoleum to carpet. Some unique ways to separate space include using an usher's rope, a free-standing lattice structure, bamboo curtains, or fabric panels. You may also set interest areas apart by using elevated places, such as a loft or a low platform. All these techniques for separating space share the goals of creating a child-scaled classroom, helping children to focus on a specific activity, and reducing the sense of crowding that may accompany being part of a large group

Pathways

In planning the location of the different interest areas, early educators must consider the best way to guide the children from one area to another. Pathways should exist between areas, allowing children to see their choices and to access areas of interest while providing protection for other interest centers. For example, pathways around the block-building center protect children's works-in-progress from children who are walking through to another interest area.

Places to Pause

Just as pathways assist children in moving about the room and previewing activity choices, sometimes children need a "place to pause" (Isbell and Exelby 2001), a private space to rest and consider what they would like to do next. When there is no physical provision for privacy, children may mentally filter out or ignore unwanted contact. Essentially, they are inwardly "spacing out" and withdrawing from the classroom. When classrooms provide specific areas that allow a child to look out a window, look at a book, or engage in a positive activity alone, a child need not expend emotional energy to protect herself. Some teachers take advantage of unique existing features of their classroom to create private space. For example, a fireplace and hearth can be painted, carpeted, and furnished with books and pillows to create a cozy nook for one or two children. A simple tent can be created by draping a blanket over a small overturned table or between two pieces of classroom furniture. With a flashlight, children will have a quiet spot to explore. Even a large cardboard box can serve children's need to be in a small space, separate from the group.

63

The View from the Lesson Plan

As the architect of the learning centers, you have the role of planning the centers, observing the children as they work and play, serving as a resource to the children in their play, and evaluating how well the centers are working for the children (Isbell 1995). Some of the learning centers you plan will be permanent features of the classroom, and they will always be available to the children. Even though these learning centers are permanent, they are not stagnant. Throughout the year, enrich the existing centers by adding new materials and thereby retaining the children's interest and stimulating more-complex play. How many centers do you need? According to the Early Childhood Environment Rating Scale (Harms, Clifford, and Cryer 1998), children should have access to at least five interest centers.

In addition to providing permanent learning centers, you will want to plan for interest centers that relate to a specific topic you are teaching. After a classroom demonstration of sinking and floating, set up a center that allows children to keep exploring those concepts. By demonstrating the possibilities for exploration that exist in the center, you give children ideas that launch their learning.

Children need sufficient time for self-directed learning in the interest centers so that the children can become deeply engaged in self-chosen activities. In general, a longer-lasting, more-focused experience in one or two centers has more value for children than a flitting visit to all of them. Children need a minimum of 30 minutes for sustained play. When the schedule allows 45 minutes to an hour, more in-depth play can take place (Isbell 1995).

The View from 2½ Feet

You've taken a big-picture look at your learning centers, noting how they're arranged in your classroom. Now it's time to inspect your learning centers from the perspective of children, evaluating what children will find in each center and determining how the materials in the center can best be displayed to capture interest.

Typical Interest Centers and Supporting Materials

Each early education classroom should include the interest centers described below. Although these centers focus on a primary area of learning or development, children do not explore math concepts only in the math center, or have literacy experiences only in the literacy areas. Development in both numeracy and literacy also take place in the construction area, the sensory areas, and so on. The more you keep in mind the integration of children's learning, the more you can enrich and extend the opportunities in the individual centers. Of the centers described on the next seven pages, the first three—the library center, the writing center, and the listening center—are literacy centers.

Library Center

The library area should contain a variety of picture books that children can explore on their own or share with a friend, including some that reflect the themes or concepts that the children are currently learning in your class. The book center should be conducive to quiet reading. The bookshelf needs to be easily accessible and filled with plenty of engaging children's books that are regularly rotated. Also include the following items:

- large pillows
- comfortable chairs
- a plush rug
- catalogs
- classroom books created through children's dictation
- puppets
- flannel-board characters from familiar stories
- mounted photographs from magazines

Writing Center

The writing center gives children an opportunity to explore writing implements and communication tools, develop skills in these areas, and learn to appreciate the value of expressing their ideas in written form. Materials need to be well organized and attractively displayed, inviting children's participation. Materials for the writing center include the following:

- paints, brushes, easel
- colored chalk, small chalkboards with erasers
- felt-tip markers
- pencils
- paper of many sizes and colors, lined and unlined
- word cards displaying familiar words
- small alphabet chart
- stencils
- envelopes of various sizes
- index cards
- pads, notebooks
- sticky notes
- greeting cards
- carbon paper, tracing paper, stencils
- magic slate
- small whiteboards
- stamp pads, letters
- pan of sand for finger writing
- sandpaper letters and numbers
- play dough to form into letters and numbers
- flannel board with letters and numbers
- mailbox
- typewriter

Listening Center

The listening center provides a place where children can listen to stories independently, following along in the text of what they are hearing. Although this type of experience with books is no substitute for the interactive reading that occurs when a teacher reads a story, it does capture children's interest and also provides an activity that gives children some time alone, separate from the rest of the group. Listening centers should include the following equipment:

- child-operated cassette or compact disc players
- recordings of high-quality children's literature
- headphones

Children will need clear instructions in the correct use of the equipment. Players can be labeled with symbols or pictures as well as words to remind children how to use them.

Dramatic Play/Home Living Center

As children spend time in dramatic play, they develop oral language and a sense of competence. The center should include the basic furnishings that will encourage children to dramatize home and family situations. If you add props, you can adapt these furnishings to a variety of themes. The best, and often the most economical, props are real objects that children can find in their own homes. The following are examples of equipment for the home living center:

- unbreakable mirror
- dress-up clothes
- jewelry
- baby bed
- high chair
- small table, chairs
- sink
- stove
- refrigerator
- cozy rug
- telephone
- ironing board
- shopping cart
- cash register
- variety of pieces of fabric with multicultural colors and designs
- storage for food items and accessories: cereal boxes, empty vegetable cans with edges filed smooth, spice containers, real-life small pots and pans, child-size plastic cups and plates, dry sponge, small dustpan and handheld broom.

The following literacy props are not just for the writing center. They are intended to encourage children to spontaneously include writing in their pretend play, thereby reinforcing the usefulness of print:

- menus, order pad, play money
- recipes, marked measuring spoons and cups
- memo pads, envelopes, address labels
- cookbooks, telephone books

In the home living center, children can dramatize the Bible story they are learning. You can convert the space for the home living center into specific themed spaces for dramatic play if another more appropriate space is not available. With the addition of props and with minor rearrangement of the space, the children can pretend they are people with various jobs and professions, such as nurses, doctors, postal workers, carpenters, firefighters, and hairdressers. The themes for dramatic play are most effective when they follow a similarly themed field trip, connecting them with the children's real experience.

Block/Construction Center

The block/construction center should be in an area of the classroom where there is little or no through traffic. The area should have plenty of floor space where children can build, create, and play. Wooden unit blocks, in particular, are essential because they are so versatile and because children can use them in open-ended play. Research suggests that children's ability to create complex block structures predicts later mathematical ability. When children build with unit blocks, they learn the names of geometric shapes and have opportunities to explore seriating and classification. When children work on a construction project together, they learn to solve problems. They have opportunities to talk, describing their building, making plans with other children, and deciding what to add next. When you invest in a set of unit blocks, it is wise to purchase well-made ones. They should be modular (that is, all sets match and have the same dimensions and proportions). The set of blocks should be large enough to allow children to create elaborate constructions. In addition to the wooden unit blocks, the center should include other blocks that are a variety of shapes and sizes so that the children can make flat structures and three-dimensional ones. The following materials will help create an engaging block/construction center:

- props
  - people
  - animals
  - trucks
  - cars
  - boats
  - airplanes
  - signs
  - car floor mat

- unit blocks
- large hollow wooden blocks
- foam blocks
- waffle blocks

Manipulatives Center

The manipulatives center should have materials that are appropriate for the children's level of development in eye-hand coordination, body dexterity, and problem solving. Materials to put together and take apart give children opportunities to develop their small muscles. These materials include the following:

- blocks that balance or connect
- large beads for stringing
- forms and shapes
- "pegboards" and pegs
- form puzzles
- wooden puzzles
- magnetic shapes
- matching and bingo games
- pipe fittings

- nuts and bolts
- Lego and Duplo blocks
- locks with keys
- nested boxes
- items for sorting: buttons, rocks, shells
- tongs and cotton balls
- eyedroppers

Music Center

In the music center the children can explore sounds made with objects of different sizes and shapes. They can listen to various types of music, including music from other cultures and music of different styles—Christian worship music, hymns, folk ballads, classical music, jazz, and so on. The music center should have a variety of musical instruments and materials that will allow children to create and experiment with sound and rhythm. Items for the music center include the following:

- homemade or commercially available instruments
- wind chimes
- cassette and tape player/CD player and CDs
- diverse recordings (regularly rotated)
- creative-movement props, such as scarves and streamers

Art/Creative-Expression Center

The art center should provide opportunities for children to create, experiment, practice skills, release feelings, and express themselves. When children spend time in the art center, they gain a sense of confidence through the many opportunities to make decisions and implement their ideas. A daily craft or art project does not take the place of an art center. The art center should encourage free expression. The only direction the teacher gives there should be explanations of the different media she brings in for the children to use. In other words, the art center should be totally child directed. The art center needs to be near the water source in the classroom. The art center should have the following items available at all times:

- scissors (child-size, left- and right-handed)
- paper (manila paper, construction paper, coffee filters, newsprint, wax paper, textured papers, cardboard)
- sticky dots
- crayons
- colored chalk
- watercolor paint
- hole punches
- tape
- markers of various sizes
- yarn
- glue and glue brushes (can be old watercolor brushes or child-size glue brushes)
- staplers
- cloth fabric
- feathers
- clay
- felt pieces
- craft sticks
- pencils
- paints
- easels
- painting smocks

Science Center

The science center should stretch the minds and imaginations of children as they discover some of the wonders of God's world. Here, children can learn about the natural environment, experiment and try out their ideas, and develop problem-solving and questioning skills. The items in the science center should change regularly and may reflect the current season. Children should be encouraged to bring in found items, both from the playground and from their experiences away from school. The following materials will introduce science in ways that captivate children:

- thermometer
- flashlight
- prism
- magnifying glass
- magnets
- plants
- animals
- fish
- insects
- shells
- grain

- variety of seeds
- dried leaves, flowers
- bird nests
- rocks
- feathers
- plastic tubing
- funnels
- eyedroppers
- clear plastic jars with lids
- aquarium
- cooking equipment

Sensory Center

When children spend time exploring sand, water, and other sensory materials, they gain small-motor coordination. They learn by experimenting with materials and by exploring the physical properties of various objects and substances. The sensory center may include the following materials:

- goop (cornstarch, water, food coloring)
- shaving cream
- oatmeal

- cornstarch
- sawdust
- flour
- play dough

- accessories for water play
    - funnels
    - eyedroppers
    - measuring cups
    - containers for pouring
    - boats
    - fish
    - people

- sand or rice tub
    - containers of all sizes
    - scoops for pouring
    - measuring cups
    - funnels
    - objects
    - plastic bugs and animals

Math Center

Children's experiences with materials in the math center will give them the opportunity to weigh, measure, count, evaluate, calculate, and much more. The math center should include diverse materials, such as the following:

- variety of objects that can be sorted, grouped, and counted
- cash register
- counting cubes and bears
- number games
- lotto games
- abacus
- egg timer
- stopwatch
- number cards
- scale
- thermometer
- play money
- rulers
- tactile number cards
- magnetic numbers and magnet board
- parquetry blocks and other objects that teach geometric shapes

This article consists primarily of information from *Early Education Director's Manual* by Debi Lydic, Debbi Keeler, and Leanne Leak (Colorado Springs, CO: Purposeful Design Publications, 2007). You may order a copy of the manual by calling ACSI Customer Service at 800-367-0798.

References

Harms, Thelma, Richard M. Clifford, and Debby Cryer. 1998. *Early childhood environment rating scale.* Rev. ed. New York: Teachers College Press.

Isbell, Rebecca. 1995. *The complete learning center book: An illustrated guide for 32 different early childhood learning centers.* Beltsville, MD: Gryphon House.

Isbell, Rebecca, and Betty Exelby. 2001. *Early learning environments that work.* Beltsville, MD: Gryphon House.

Kritchevsky, Sybil, Elizabeth Prescott, and Lee Walling. 1977. *Planning environments for young children: Physical space.* 2nd ed. Washington, DC: National Association for the Education of Young Children.

REFLECTION

Twos and Threes Need Centers Too!

By Stacia Emerson. Reprinted from *CEE*, November 2007.

Walk into a typical kindergarten or preschool classroom and it will become obvious that the room is set up in centers, or areas for specific learning activities to take place. But what about toddlers? Not as many classrooms for twos and threes have designated learning centers. It could be that these centers seem a bit too structured for the toddlers, but that doesn't have to be the case. Setting up the toddler classroom into centers, or play areas, will provide consistency for the schedule while providing flexibility and accommodating for the attention span of the toddlers. Below you will find general guidelines that are helpful for creating centers in a toddler classroom. The chart that follows the guidelines shows information about specific centers that are appropriate for toddlers.

Guidelines for Arranging Play Areas (Centers)

1. Place the quiet areas together and the noisy areas together.
2. Place messy areas near the sink or the bathroom.
3. Keep materials organized and stored near the area. Labeled boxes or plastic containers work well.
4. Label shelves with pictures, and teach children how to put materials away. Cut pictures from catalogs for labels.
5. Introduce materials before you place them in a play area. Demonstrate how to use the materials and how to care for them. Show the children where the materials will be stored so that they can participate in cleanup. You can do these introductory activities in a brief circle time.
6. Allow children time to explore the new materials. During center time, a teacher may need to monitor that area closely to reinforce proper use of the materials.
7. Post a description of the educational value of the center. Doing so not only helps parents and volunteers understand the purpose you are trying to accomplish but also allows them to participate with you.

Learning Centers for Twos and Threes

	Purpose	Materials	Literacy Promotion
Manipulative/Fine-Motor Center	To develop and practice fine-motor and perceptual motor skills such as grasping, releasing, inserting, twisting, turning, pushing, pulling, assembling, and disassembling	Puzzles, play dough, toys that have movable parts such as knobs and dials, shape sorters, musical instruments, lacing cards, beads for stringing	• Include paper, crayons, and other materials for writing and drawing. • Add an alphabet chart for a print model. • Add pictures of children working (encourages oral language development). • For threes, set up a separate writing center, bingo, and memory games. • Use logos from coupons to create game cards • Encourage graphing and sorting.
Dramatic Play Center	• To develop and practice role-playing, creative dynamics, social interaction, and fine-motor skills • To interact with print and see how print is used in everyday life • To learn how God wants us to treat others in His world • To gain appreciation for differences in other cultures such as in clothing, simple traditions, and food choices • To gain appreciation for differences in families as reflected in homes that contain adopted children, single parents, and grandparents as guardians	Playhouse; dolls, doll clothes, doll bed, and similar items; kitchen props such as a stove, a sink, dishes, and utensils; dress-up clothes; child-size furniture; props for playing roles such as teacher, doctor, and storekeeper; props such as hats, clothes, and utensils that are representative of various cultures	• Include paper, notepads, pencils, crayons, junk mail, coupons, logos, catalogs, magazines, old phone books, menus, and similar items. • Add books related to families, jobs, and other cultures. • Display charts of text such as songs and poems. • Add photos of children and families (for oral-language development). • Use empty food containers to let the children see print.

	Purpose	Materials	Literacy Promotion
Art/Messy Center	• To discover colors, shapes, and textures • To experiment informally with a variety of simple media • To express ideas through ways such as picture making and constructing • To learn about the senses—especially sight and touch—that God gave them, and how they use them to explore God's world	Various kinds of paper, crayons, pencils, washable markers, paint, easel, sand/water table, chalk, smocks	• Always have materials for drawing. • Label the items in the center. • Use children's photos in the center.
Blocks/Vehicle Center	• To develop and practice fine- and large-motor skills, social interaction skills, and problem-solving skills	Blocks, various building sets, and related figures such as cars, trucks, boats, animals, people, buildings, and traffic signs	• Include paper and crayons for drawing pictures. • Display posters, signs, and logos so that the children can see print. • Put related books in the center (e.g., *Truck* by Donald Crews).*

Library/Quiet Center	• To have opportunities to
	  ◦ listen to stories
	  ◦ increase vocabulary
	  ◦ interpret pictures
	  ◦ develop imagination
	  ◦ interact with others
	• To learn about Bible truths by listening to stories from the Bible
		Books, cassette tapes or CDs of stories, small chairs, pictures, puppets and props for storytelling, charts displaying text such as poems and songs, and comfortable places to sit that include items such as pillows	• Include teacher-made and student-made books.
			• Label the items in the center.
			• Add walk-on stories.
			• Provide a place for children to use simple props to retell and dramatize stories (teacher may need to be present).
			• Have an adult sit and explore books with the children.

Large-Motor Center	• To develop and practice large-motor and perceptual-motor skills such as bending, stretching, walking, hopping, squatting, balancing, and practicing coordination • To learn how God created them to be unique and special	Slides, tunnel, riding toys, push toys, rocking boat, balls, pictures, and charts	• Sing action songs with the children. • Encourage oral language by having children verbalize about their movements. • Read books that encourage movement (e.g., *From Head to Toe* by Eric Carle).** • This center could be a place for active dramatization.

*Donald Crews. 1980. *Truck*. New York: Greenwillow Books.
**Eric Carle. 1999. *From Head to Toe*. Board book ed. New York: HarperFestival.

REFLECTION

Self-Evaluation Tool: Learning Centers

By Leanne Leak. Reprinted from *CEE*, November 2007.

Walk through your classroom and take inventory of the adequacy and variety of your learning centers. Observe the children at play and evaluate how well your centers are helping them fully engage in play and learning.

Room Arrangement

Yes No

☐ ☐ **Quiet play areas** (reading corner and listening center) are separated from active, noisy play areas (construction center and dramatic play center).

☐ ☐ **Boundaries** separate the learning centers so that the centers are clearly defined.

☐ ☐ **Pathways** guide children as they move from one learning center to another.

Assessment of Teacher's Behavior

Rarely Inconsistently Consistently

☐ ☐ ☐ I rotate the materials displayed in each learning center, changing them as needed to correlate with learning themes and to maintain children's interest.

☐ ☐ ☐ I modify the learning centers on the basis of my observations of children at play.

☐ ☐ ☐ I respond to the children's ideas and suggestions for modifying the learning centers.

☐ ☐ ☐ I plan the daily schedule to give children sufficient time (45 minutes to one hour) for sustained play.

Quantity

How many play spaces are available for each child?

Number of play spaces: _____

Number of children: _____

Number of play spaces per child: 0   ½   1   1½   2   2½   3

Place a yes (Y) or a no (N) below in the four empty boxes for each center listed at the left.

Availability—Is this center available at your center?

Appeal—The display of the materials allows the children to see their choices easily. The shelves are not overcrowded.

Accessibility—The arrangement of the materials allows the children to select an activity independently and return the materials afterward.

Stimulation/Challenge—The center includes materials that provide various levels of difficulty so that children who have diverse capabilities can experience success (e.g., puzzles with few pieces and puzzles with many pieces).

	Availability	Appeal	Accessibility	Stimulation/ Challenge
Library				
Writing				
Listening				
Dramatic Play/ Home Living				
Block/Construction				
Music				
Manipulatives				
Art				
Science				
Sensory				
Math				

On the basis of whether you indicated a yes or a no in the boxes, you may want to think about how to expand what you offer or increase the likelihood of engaging the children.

Nature **A**ppreciation

By Stacia Emerson. Reprinted from *CEE*, March 2009.

If we want preschoolers to develop an appreciation for art, we expose them to different types and forms of art, we invite artists into our classrooms, and we visit museums. If we want them to appreciate music, we play different kinds of music in the classroom, and we invite musicians to come and play. So it follows with nature and the environment. To develop a love for the world that God created and an understanding of how to care for it, children must spend time exploring it.

Because young children learn best by doing and by involving all their senses, it is important that teachers provide these kinds of experiences when teaching about the environment and ecology. Children should not just hear about what they need to do to take care of God's world; they should actually participate. At a young age, children can develop lifelong habits that benefit them, their families, their communities, and the entire world! Each person *can* make a difference!

Developing these habits and an appreciation for our environment takes more than just a unit around Earth Day each year. Early educators can easily integrate concepts about nature and ecology into daily classroom life and weekly unit plans. Commonly taught units such as the following can focus on environmental issues and therefore provide year-round teaching on the subject: seasons, senses (what we see, hear, smell, and feel in the environment), community helpers (jobs related to the environment), weather, zoo animals (endangered animals, caring for animals), farm life, and pets. Most of the concepts relate to science, and early educators can easily adapt them to meet young children's needs for active, sensory-based learning. The chart on the next page shows how to make nature concepts come to life for young children.

You as early educators can teach these concepts all year long. Your modeling and active participation are both necessary for children to develop an understanding of the importance of caring for our world (Eliason and Jenkins 2003). For this teaching to be effective, make sure that children have plenty of unstructured time to spend outdoors exploring and messing around in the environment. It seems that children spend less and less time outdoors, so giving them time to explore nature while they are at school is even more important than in the past. Teach children how to observe, appreciate, and care for all that God has given us.

Concepts	Experiences
Reduce, reuse, and recycle.	• Set up recycle bins at school for plastic, paper, and aluminum. • Decorate canvas bags to use for lunches. • Emphasize reusable lunch containers for lunches instead of paper and plastic bags. • Decorate reusable bags for trash to put in cars, use at home, and use in other locations. • Start a compost pile. • Do craft projects by using discarded materials such as cardboard tubes, magazines, wallpaper, books, fabric scraps, paper scraps, and wood scraps. Explain why you reuse or recycle these things. • Set up a swap/exchange box to bring things from home that are not needed anymore such as clothes, shoes, toys, and books. • Have a paper-scrap box in the classroom, and encourage children to use it as much as possible.
Nature—God's creation—is interesting and always changing.	• Adopt a tree: take photos and draw pictures of it in different seasons, have picnics under it, put bird feeders on it, write about it, and care for it. • Observe nature: make a circle on the grass by using yarn, and observe what is in the circle; bird watch; plant a butterfly garden, and observe the garden. • Create a nature center by collecting objects such as nuts, shells, and rocks. Allow time for activities such as observing, drawing, sorting, and touching. • Start nature journals: ask children to draw and write about things they observe in nature.
Living things need to be cared for and protected.	• Bring in caterpillars, and observe the life cycle of butterflies. • Care for a class pet such as a fish or a bird. • Care for plants in the classroom. • Learn how to protect plants and animals in their natural environment. • Visit nearby parks frequently, and observe how the environment is cared for or not cared for.
The quality of our air, water, and soil is determined by how we take care of them.	• Start a litter patrol in the school's area; encourage families to start one in their areas. • Learn how to conserve water while brushing teeth, washing a car, showering, and doing other such activities.

Reference

Eliason, Claudia, and Loa Jenkins. 2003. *A practical guide to early childhood curriculum.* 7th ed. Upper Saddle River, NJ: Prentice Hall.

Doing Math in the Block Center

By Joyce Eady Myers. Reprinted from *CEE*, March 2008.

My first kindergarten classroom was a large, well-equipped room located in a local church building. In the corner of the carpeted area there was a shelf of unit blocks. The blocks were a constant source of irritation to me. Every Monday and Thursday morning, I needed to arrive early to straighten up the "mess" left from the previous evening's church activities. During center time, I was concerned that several children only wanted to play with the blocks and never wanted to participate in other activities. One little guy took great pleasure in building towers and knocking them over repeatedly. Quite honestly, I did not have a clue what to do with the blocks. I knew that every early childhood classroom should have them, but they were just a necessary nuisance in my classroom.

We find the first description of today's alphabet blocks in the essay *Some Thoughts Concerning Education* by John Locke. Friedrich Froebel, the "father of the kindergarten," developed a system of gifts and occupations that were used in his curriculum in Germany. Gifts two through six were blocks. Blocks have been a fixture in early education since the nineteenth century. However, the unit blocks of the twenty-first-century classroom come from the work of Caroline Pratt, an early-twentieth-century teacher in the United States. Despite the historical legacy of blocks, most teachers think of blocks only as a play center, thus missing wonderful teaching opportunities.

Unit blocks, which provide superb hands-on math experience, are an example of play's value for mathematical learning. They offer a standard proportion (1:2:4) that promotes children's understanding of mathematical relationships. Through using unit blocks, children have concrete encounters with a number of mathematical concepts such as area, size, shape, space, numbers, patterns, measuring, fractions, estimating, one-to-one correspondence, counting, adding, and subtracting.

Focal Points

What can you as an early education professional do to promote intentional mathematical experiences in the block center? First of all, you need to know and understand the curriculum focal points from the Principles and Standards for School

Mathematics developed by the National Council of Teachers of Mathematics (http://standards.nctm.org). The curriculum focal points are as follows: (1) number and operations, (2) geometry, and (3) measurement. In addition, most states have early learning standards that address concepts that children must be introduced to in the preschool years.

Math Talk

Second, you can be intentional in your use of "math talk" in the classroom. Recent research suggests that the amount of teachers' math-related talk significantly relates to the growth of preschoolers' conventional mathematical knowledge over the school year (Klibanoff et al. 2006). You can purposefully use words related to mathematics as you observe and interact with children who are playing and working in the block center. You can use the correct names of shapes, use scaffolding techniques, and ask mathematical questions about the structures that children build.

Let's take a visit to Mrs. Mitchell's class of four-year-olds and observe center time in the block corner. Mrs. Mitchell has arranged the unit blocks on the shelves by shape. She has labeled each shelf with a picture-and-word sign that tells the shape. When the children clean up, they categorize the blocks by shape and put them back on the shelves neatly. For example, as Joshua was cleaning up, Mrs. Mitchell said to him, "Joshua, thank you for putting all the rectangles together on the shelf."

On the wall next to the shelf we notice a word chart. Mrs. Mitchell and the children have been working together to add words to the chart, which describes the blocks. Words that Mrs. Mitchell has written on the word chart describe not only the blocks but also the structures that the children have built. The word chart displays words such as *corner*, *edge*, *hard*, *flat*, *tall*, *square*, *rectangle*, *ramp*, *many*, *more than*, and *less than*. During the school year, Mrs. Mitchell and the children will continue to add words to the chart.

Numbers and Shapes

Mrs. Mitchell points out a new box on the shelf. It contains laminated cards that display pictures of the various block shapes. Morgan is sitting on the floor matching the correct block shape to the cards. She is developing an understanding of one-to-one correspondence as she plays the "block game." Mrs. Mitchell has placed under the word chart several baskets labeled with numbers. This week the numbers are 7, 8, 9, and 10. Travis and Jordan are working together, counting and placing the correct number of blocks in the baskets. Jordan calls to Mrs. Mitchell and says, "Look, teacher, there are more blocks in the 10 basket than in the 9 basket." Mrs. Mitchell responds by saying, "Yes, that's correct; 10 is more than 9." She is reinforcing the concept of number and operations.

In the center of the carpeted block area we see the outline of a square that Mrs. Mitchell has made with masking tape. The class is learning about squares this month, and Mrs. Mitchell wants to reinforce the concept. As Ian and Chloe start to play, Mrs. Mitchell says, "Today we are going to build inside the square." The children are learning about geometry and spatial sense. To extend the activity, Mrs. Mitchell encourages Ian and Chloe to see what they can build using only the square blocks. Of course, Mrs. Mitchell will regularly rotate and change the activities in the block center.

Reinforcing Activities

The activities in Mrs. Mitchell's classroom reinforce the concepts of number and operations and geometry. What about measurement? While playing in the block center, children can also investigate measurement concepts. What can you as their teacher do to encourage them to investigate?

Children like to measure items. Guide them to measure objects and places using blocks. The following are some suggestions for measuring:

- Help children draw an outline of themselves on butcher paper. Measure the outline with blocks. The children can then tell "how many blocks" tall they are.
- Measure a table in the room with blocks.
- Measure the length of the block center.

In addition to enjoying the exploration of length, children will enjoy discovering the weight of blocks. Place a balance scale in the block center and allow the children to discover which blocks balance with each other and which blocks are the heaviest.

Preschool classrooms can contain many other types of blocks such as Duplos, table blocks, Bristle Blocks, and snap blocks. These smaller blocks can give children great opportunities to explore patterns. When children recognize and duplicate simple sequential patterns, they are learning the foundational knowledge of algebra. Use these ideas to have children combine blocks and patterns:

- Make pattern cards on 8x10 heavy paper, and laminate the cards for durability. The children can use the blocks to re-create the patterns on the cards.
- Create patterns on adding machine tape. Put the adding machine tape in a basket of snap blocks. The children can duplicate the patterns they see on the tape.
- The children can make patterns by looking at paper shapes and working with a partner to re-create the patterns using table blocks.

You can add another dimension to your block center by integrating blocks with math and literature. You can link stories to the block area. After listening to the story of Humpty Dumpty, the children can use blocks to build the wall. Encourage the children to measure the wall as well as to use spatial words to describe the wall. After you read to them *The Three Billy Goats Gruff* (Galdone 1973), the children can play by retelling the story in the block area. They can build the bridge using triangles and arches. You can ask open-ended questions, prompting the children to use words such as *under* and *over*.

Blocks continue to be a favorite activity of many preschool children. Through organizing, planning, and intentionally using math words, you can ensure that the children are learning important math concepts while they are enjoying the block center. Through the years, I have learned about the block center and the learning that takes place when children are engaged there. It is no longer a necessary nuisance but an integral part of the learning experience in my classroom.

References

Galdone, Paul. 1973. *The three billy goats gruff.* New York: Clarion Books.

Klibanoff, Raquel S., Susan C. Levine, Janellen Huttenlocher, Marina Vasilyeva, and Larry V. Hedges. 2006. Preschool children's mathematical knowledge: The effect of teacher "math talk." *Developmental Psychology* 42, no. 1 (January): 59–69.

Additional Reading

Chalufour, Ingrid, and Karen Worth. 2004. *Building structures with young children.* St. Paul, MN: Redleaf Press.

Hirsch, Elisabeth S., ed. 1996. *The block book.* 3rd ed. Washington, DC: National Association for the Education of Young Children.

MacDonald, Sharon. 2001. *Block play: The complete guide to learning and playing with blocks.* Beltsville, MD: Gryphon House.

Wellhousen, Karyn, and Judith Kieff. 2001. *A constructivist approach to block play in early childhood.* Albany, NY: Delmar.

Imagination Challenged? Have We Got an Idea for You!

By the *CEE* Staff. Reprinted from *CEE*, May 2009.

Jesus, famous for making interesting comments, made a statement that continues to make us pause: "Unless you change and become like little children, you will never enter the kingdom of heaven (Matthew 18:3). Over the years, theologians have commented on what Jesus meant. There's another way to unpack the mystery of this Scripture: observe children—notice what gives them joy, how they respond in situations, what their common characteristics are—then determine if your life reflects any of those observations.

In thinking on this Scripture, many take away this thought: children are trusting, and we adults need to be more trusting of our heavenly Father. Others take away the idea that children are quick to forgive and that adults need to adopt the same posture. But I wonder whether Jesus was also referring to the insatiable curiosity of children. What would happen if we adults were overwhelmingly curious about the things of God? What if we adults leaned into our birthright of creativity and continually found more ways to serve humankind (think penicillin and air travel) and more ways to spread the gospel (think Gutenberg's printing press and the Internet).

The Challenge

As a team, we realized that it's not enough to have good ideas. We need the fortitude to bring those ideas into reality—a process that often takes more creativity than the ideas themselves. We need to *nurture* our creativity in tangible ways. Have you ever heard educators bemoan the fact that human beings are at the height of creativity as children and that they slowly lose that ability as they get older? We put ourselves on a crash course to interrupt that trend. We came up with the imagination challenge and invited some colleagues to join us.

The following chart explains the imagination challenge, which consists of four parts: preparation, journaling activities, field trips, and extension activities.

85

Preparation	• Fast from media. • Meet in a new environment. • Commit to blind participation.
Journaling Activities	Three journaling activities take place throughout the challenge in order to engage each participant and gauge the individual responses toward a renewed perspective.
Field Trips	The facilitator's guide lists suggestions for group outings that you can do at little or no cost.
Extension Activities	Even in a group, we learn as individuals. We've included some additional activities so that you can continue to pursue the growth of creativity and imagination.

Check out some of these responses to the challenge:

Do you give yourself time to be creative?

- "Only when a situation comes available for work or when helping others."

- "Not really. Often, work and tasks at home take precedence."

- "I have to. It's just a part of me; without it I feel empty and sad."

- "Yes, as needed within reason."

How do these activities benefit others you serve? Coworkers? Friends? Family?

- "I am creating and sharing ideas. It might benefit my coworkers."

- "I think I would be a calmer person! I think I would also take more time connecting and less time being task oriented. Lastly, I think the more I am conscious about exploring my creative side, the more I can be creative in my work."

- "I think the biggest benefit was team building—learning something new together and learning about one another."

Do you feel inspired to find more time to be creative? Why or why not?

"[The challenge] reminded me that I need to be more intentional with taking time to be more creative, to create space for me to think outside the box."

What Others Are Saying

Bonnie Neugebauer reminds us of the importance of relearning playfulness as adults. What are you willing to surrender in order to embrace the benefits of playfulness, which closely ties with creativity? Consider the following points by Neugebauer (Child Care Information Exchange 2009):

Time. Play requires a sense of timelessness. The outcome of play is secondary to the process of play. Those playing must be able to continue the experience across blocks of time.

Sense of self. Play requires forgetting oneself. If people are self-conscious as they try to play, feeling concern about how others will view their play or its products, then those people are crippled in their attempts to play.

Sense of order. Play requires some chaos. People need to have an awareness that they can use things and do things in new ways. Players need a sense of uncertainty, and they need support for taking risks.

Joy. Play that lacks enjoyment is simply hard work. Players must laugh, and they must practice playing. Play brings out the best in people.

The Imagination Challenge

Do you need to take the imagination challenge? Take this short questionnaire and see where you fall:

Yes   No

☐   ☐   Do you always visit the same locations, such as restaurants, parks, and shops, in your community?

☐   ☐   Do you have the exact same routine each week?

☐   ☐   Have you had the same hairstyle for the last three years?

☐   ☐   Are you bored with your personal devotions?

☐   ☐   Does your schedule consist of the same activities and no flexibility?

☐   ☐   Do you use the same lesson plans or on-site staff trainings every year?

☐   ☐   Do you always read the same devotional book during your quiet times?

☐   ☐   Does buying trendy styles overwhelm you?

☐   ☐   Is it hard for you to stop and talk with someone because doing so disrupts your schedule?

☐   ☐   When you walk around in your house, are you are no longer conscious of the pictures or the decorations because they are just part of the background?

☐   ☐   Have you stopped asking questions about your faith?

☐   ☐   Do you rarely or never change the decorations in your work space?

☐ ☐ Do you rotate the same meals week after week for yourself or your family?

☐ ☐ Do you always drive the same way home?

☐ ☐ Do you always shop at the same store for your clothing and accessories?

Total all your yeses. What does your total indicate you should do?

All yeses	Stop what you are doing right now and begin the challenge.
11–14 yeses	Find a friend who will challenge your routine; then do some activities together.
6–10 yeses	Look at some of the personal activities on the challenge and expand what you're doing.
1–5 yeses	You're in a great place. Encourage others around you to be adventurous.
No yeses	You could lead an imagination challenge, so find others to join you!

It's Your Turn

If you think you want to participate in an activity that would cause you to mirror the responses above, download *CEE*'s imagination challenge, and prepare to be inspired! Go to www.acsi.org, and search for "imagination challenge" to download the six-page facilitator's guide to the imagination challenge. Use the guide with your staff, your coworkers, and even your family. And remember, new environments + new experiences = new perspectives.

Reference
Child Care Information Exchange. 2009. Review of the article The spirit of adult play. ExchangeEveryDay. January 15. http://www.childcareexchange.com/eed/issue.php?id=2169.

Sponges: Children and Language

By Stacia Emerson. Reprinted from *CEE*, March 2007.

Children have been compared to many things through the years in an attempt to describe their personalities, their potential, or their development. For example, it has been said that children come to us as blank slates or as sponges, ready to take in everything from their environment.

Regarding the acquisition of language, it is easy to view an infant's brain as a sponge. From the very beginning of their life, infants are soaking up the language from their environment. They are learning their parents' soothing voices. They respond to songs, familiar faces, and conversations around them. In fact, research has concluded over and over that a child's brain is programmed for its greatest learning potential in language during the first four or five years of life. So these years are the critical years for language learning, and this is the time when language is most easily and effectively learned. Therefore, early childhood teachers must take advantage of the time they have with children and use it effectively for language learning.

The Four Language Modes

	Receptive Language	Expressive Language
Primary (oral)	Listening	Speaking
Secondary (written)	Reading	Writing

The table above gives a concise picture of the order in which children learn the language arts. Initially children are taking in language (receptive). During this time, adults should be talking to children about everything. Children are learning what language is, that words have meaning, and that things happen as a result of language. Once their physical development allows them to, children begin speaking (expressive). Usually around two years of age, toddlers begin using the vocabulary they have been exposed to previously. If infants have been in a language-rich environment, they will have much to talk about when the time comes! Those first two years are a big part of the foundation for the rest of language learning.

The following lists contain practical ways that teachers can encourage receptive and expressive language development in young children during these critical years of language learning. The use of these techniques throughout the routines of the day will help create a language-rich environment for young children.

Vocabulary Development (Receptive Language)

- Speak slowly to infants in short sentences. Use a singsong voice to get their attention while looking them in the face.
- Talk through routine situations, explaining what you are doing: "I am mixing up your bottle, and then you will get something good to eat."
- Talk about what the child is doing: "You are pushing one block on the floor. You like how it sounds. Now you are pushing two blocks."
- When a child uses telegraphic speech or one-word sentences, expound on the language. If the child says, "Blankie," you respond, "You need your blankie now. It is so soft and warm."
- Share concept books and picture books containing objects that a child can name.
- Be patient as children try to use language themselves. Give them time.
- Take the time to listen to toddlers. Their speech can be slow, but don't speak for them.
- Label objects in the child's environment with pictures and words. The labels will give you opportunities for discussions.
- Be a language partner with toddlers. Encourage even the shy children to have conversations with you.

Sound and Print Awareness (Receptive and Expressive Language)

- Read books to infants (it is never too early!). Use books that contain bright colors and simple pictures.
- Allow infants and toddlers to manipulate board books and books made of cloth and plastic.
- As you show the picture books, discuss what you see: "Look at the puppy. He's a brown, furry puppy."

- Allow children to turn the pages as you read. Show them how to hold the book.
- Make time to read books to children every day.
- Let children "read" the stories by telling you what they remember. These approximations are important in their future reading success.

Writing Exploration (Expressive Language)

- Label children's cubbies and belongings with their names.
- Label other materials in the room with names and pictures.
- Provide materials for drawing and scribbling such as large crayons, markers, large chalk, and plenty of sturdy paper. Toddlers and twos love to explore these.
- Give children opportunities to see you writing as you make lists, signs, or labels. Talk about what you are doing.

(Dodge, Rudick, and Berke 2006)

These techniques are easy to implement in an early childhood setting. But they don't just happen. Teachers must set language goals for the children in their care; teachers must also be intentional about their methods of reaching the goals. These methods must be included in planning the day to make them effective for each child's learning potential. Teachers must be "pouring out" language all day for these little "sponges" to soak up!

Reference

Dodge, Diane Trister, Sherrie Rudick, and Kai-Leé Berke. 2006. Building language and literacy skills in infants, toddlers and twos. Teaching Strategies. http://www.teachingstrategies.com/pages/article.cfm?articleID=75.

Additional Reading

Hubbard, Michelle. 2006. Engaging story books for infants and toddlers [a listing]. Hubbard's Cupboard. http://www.hubbardscupboard.org.

Raines, Shirley, Karen Miller, and Leah Curry-Rood. 2002. *Story s-t-r-e-t-c-h-e-r-s for infants, toddlers, and twos: Experiences, activities, and games for popular children's books*. Beltsville, MD: Gryphon House.

Section 4 Authors

Stacia Emerson, PhD, has served in multiple roles within early education: a teacher, a Sunday school teacher, and a college professor. She is currently a professor at Texas Wesleyan University.

Leanne Leak, BA, serves as ACSI's western states early education field director. Leanne is conversant in early education policy and accreditation, and she maintains her knowledge base in early education through continual reading, synthesis, and study. She is in the process of completing a graduate degree.

Joyce Eady Myers has a doctorate in early childhood education from the University of North Texas. Joyce has worked with children for 35 years as a mother, a public school teacher, an international missionary, a children's minister, and a Christian school principal. She received an AB degree from Mercer University in Macon, Georgia. Joyce teaches university classes in education in the Dallas-Fort Worth area and enjoys teaching professional development sessions to teachers in faith-based schools. She and her husband live in Plano, Texas, and they have two young-adult sons.

92

Section 5:
Technology

Digital Immigrants Teaching Digital Natives: Educating in a Flat World

By D'Arcy Maher. Reprinted from *CEE*, May 2008.

I'm a digital immigrant. This fact is reinforced when I use my digital camera, program my iPod, or change the settings on my cell phone. I approach these tasks with a little tinge of fear that I will forget what to do, cause the program to crash, or just break the thing. I envy the digital native.

Facts

- Perspectives on computer use in the young child classroom differ widely.
- Technology continually changes.
- Technology encompasses much more than computer use.
- Instructional materials for technology in early education classrooms are scarce and not well constructed.

Question

What is our responsibility toward teaching today's children, who will function in a digital world?

Defining the Terms

A *digital immigrant* is "an individual who grew up without digital technology and adopted it later." The term comes from "an analogy to a country's natives, for whom the local religion, language, and folkways are natural and indigenous, over against immigrants to a country who must adapt and assimilate to their newly adopted home." In fact, "digital immigrants are said to have a 'thick accent' when operating in the digital world in distinctly pre-digital ways, when, for instance, he might 'dial' someone on the telephone to ask if his e-mail was received" (Wikipedia).

A *digital native* is "a person who has grown up with digital technology such as computers, the Internet, mobile phones and MP3." But "not everyone agrees with the language and underlying assumptions of the *digital native*, particularly as it pertains to the concept of their differentiation. There are many reasonable arguments against this differentiation. It suggests a fluidity with technology that not all children and young adults have, and a corresponding awkwardness with technology that not all older adults have. It entirely ignores the fact that the digital universe was conceived of and created by *digital immigrants*. Finally, in its application, the concept of the digital native preferences technological users as having a special status as it relates to technology because they **use it**, which glosses over the significant differences between technology users and technology creators (Wikipedia, emphasis in original).

A *flat world* is a world where individuals from every corner can compete, on equal footing, because of access to the Internet. Geography is no longer a hindrance to success, prominence, or impact.

Those just graduating from high school are digital natives. Those of us currently teaching in early education classrooms are digital immigrants. To us, the digital environment, the digital culture, is learned. The environment is less familiar; it is less natural, more intimidating. And the children currently in classrooms are digital natives. They are not intimidated in the least by technology. In fact, they perceive equipment and technology —and learning about those things—as an adventure.

Today's children will face a very different world in their adulthood. The culture will be more integrated with computers, other electronics, and gadgets. There will be more dependence on written communication (e-mail and text messages) and less necessity for personal, face-to-face interaction. It will be a place where "textality" will replace personality—where words and the use of language must be infused with so much nuance that people become recognizable by their word choices, punctuation, font selection, phrasing, and sentence construction.

Will today's children, who are following the current pioneers of the flat world, settle on the edges of the newly discovered opportunities? Or will they continue to explore and pioneer beyond our current horizons, creating not-yet-imagined opportunities and assuming occupations that are currently nameless?

What is the best way to prepare children for this kind of reality?

Create a Global Culture in Your Classroom

Futurist Andrew Zolli, in an interview in *National Geographic Traveler*, discusses how technology provides a platform for an increasingly fluid society. He paints a compelling picture:

> The Millennials, young people coming out of high school and college, are more socially connected than any generation, in part because they have digital tools to help them easily join and form social alliances. One of the by-products of increased global connectivity is that smaller groups of people can forge coherent forms of identity.... These don't have to be geographically linked. Information technology reinforces a sense of identity and actually begins to dissolve national borders. *So the next generation will increasingly blaze its travel trails electronically.* (Bellows 2007, 36; italics added)

As our children grow up in this fluid society of global connectivity, it will serve them well to be aware of, interested in, and knowledgeable about other cultures and traditions. Having experiences that connect them to individuals in other countries awakes their empathy and underscores the need to be responsible, participative members of this global village. Responsible, participative members continually ask, "What can I learn from others?" and "What can I contribute?"

Emphasize Social and Emotional Development

In a world that values efficiency through the automation of routine tasks, interpersonal skills are in high demand. That demand will only increase when automation becomes a primary delivery system of most services. Those who understand, empathize, create networks of teams, and negotiate with diverse populations will possess a skill set that cannot be digitized or automated.

Children learn to value relationships from seeing examples. Children learn appropriate social behaviors through observing and practicing. Simple behaviors such as eye contact, appropriate touch, and respectful dialogue are modeled during each warm, personal interaction. Can the children relax in your classroom? Can they be themselves, or do they fear rejection? Are they comfortable expressing emotion, or are they overly expressive? Are they learning to regulate their emotions appropriately? Can they participate as a team member—"getting along well with others"?

Encourage Language Development

Language, both oral and symbolic (written), will continue to be the primary vehicles of commerce. And yet children today spend time being entertained by passive media, which does not require interaction. When using passive media, children do not have to use live language, so they are not practicing speech. There is not a requirement to be understood. Language development, then, becomes a clear priority in the early education classroom.

Anecdotal example. My neighbor is a speech therapist at our neighborhood school. The speech therapists at the school are overwhelmed, and the school district is struggling to add more therapists to each campus. Almost every child enrolled in kindergarten needs language remediation of some kind. Most are not speaking in complete sentences, nor can they correctly pronounce the letters of the alphabet.

Prepare an Environment of Curiosity

We may not be able to conceive the world that today's children will inhabit, but we can nurture in them a skill that will transcend any environment: curiosity. Curiosity drives us to learn—whether through exploration, inquiry, or experimentation. Acting on curious thoughts encourages us to initiate, and initiation develops our work ethic.

Does your classroom encourage the children's curiosity? Do you rotate the materials? Do you encourage the children to ask questions, helping them feel that they are not interrupting? Are there materials for exploration and experimentation? Do lessons include an intentional hook for their curiosity?

Provide an Appropriate Example

Technology integration in our current culture becomes more and more prominent. There are times I just don't want to learn to use another gadget! Technology changes with a greater and greater rapidity that can soon overwhelm us. You may want to shut down and ignore the changes—or you might be on the other side of the equation, wanting to own every new piece of technology. So what is an appropriate example?

Perhaps the best word to use here is *balance*. Balance your time between personal interactions and technology-based activities. Ask yourself, Is my TV on even if I'm not watching it? How often must I check my e-mail? Balance your dependence on technology and your dependence on your own discovery. Must you run to Google with every question? Manage the technology in your life; don't let it become your master.

Focus on Spiritual Development

Because we cannot know all the changes occurring in this digital frontier in enough time to create right-and-wrong or good-and-bad checklists, the moral and spiritual formation of a child must include the knowledge of transcendent principles. Scriptural principles provide guidance in any context. Children will eventually need to develop a discerning spirit as the culture continues to evolve and shift.

There are times I am surprised that the ink in my Bible is dry. The words and lessons seem fresh and ever so applicable. They are alive! How can it be that the Sermon on the Mount seems just as relevant today as in the time that Jesus spoke the words? Those lessons will not go out of style or lose their intent. They help form the foundation on which all of life can be built.

I'm a digital immigrant. I want to support the success of the next generation. I don't want them to have any of my apprehension about technology—to fear its use. But I can't seem to share their fascination with gaming or other forms of passive media. I can go days without checking my Facebook or MySpace accounts.

I struggle to stay caught up in reading websites for research or blogs for fun. I can't seem to remember my passwords for important business accounts. Yes, I envy the digital native. How about we learn together ... deal?

Reference
Bellows, Keith. 2007. The road ahead: An expert on change ponders how global trends will impact the nature of travel. *National Geographic Traveler* 24, no. 5 (July/August): 36–39.

REFLECTION

Choosing Classroom Software

By the ACSI Technology Department. Reprinted from *CEE*, March 2007.

Technology is an integral part of our lives. Social networking (MySpace, mobile phones), music (iPods, MP3 players), and information gathering (breaking news, books online) are some examples in our technical culture. The classroom is not isolated from the influence of modern technology. For educators, it is no longer a question of whether software should be in the classroom but rather what software they should choose. There are many software products competing for the approval of educators, and technology is changing at such a rapid rate that choosing software can be a challenging task.

Educators are in the best position to know the needs of their classroom, so what follows are some guidelines to help determine the suitability of educational software. These points can assist in consistently and comprehensively evaluating software for the classroom.

3-C Educational Software Evaluation

Content

Age appropriateness

☐ Is the software developmentally, linguistically, and conceptually appropriate?

☐ Does the software support a range of age-level abilities?

Learning evaluation tool

    Does the software provide

    ☐ personalized progress tracking to both the student and the educator?

    ☐ summary reports of classroom progress for the educator?

    ☐ tangible, personalized printouts of progress for the student?

Modeling of best practices

    Is the software

    ☐ easy to install and maintain?

    ☐ easy to use by the student?

    ☐ configurable for different skill levels?

Learning activities and educational focus

    Does the software employ

    ☐ problem-solving techniques?

    ☐ open-ended problems?

    ☐ discovery-driven lessons?

    ☐ child-initiated and child-controlled activities?

    ☐ student personalization, or customization?

    ☐ multisensory stimulation, including sight, sound, and touch?

    ☐ gender, age, and race equality?

    ☐ fun, engaging activities?

Cost

Educational pricing

☐ Are discounted prices available for bulk purchases made by educators?

Licensing model

☐ Is the license student, site, or subscription based?

☐ Does the license allow for parent involvement and home use?

Internet connectivity and Web-based tools

☐ Is the software Web based or dependent on a fast Internet connection?

☐ Is the software safe and secure from intrusion, and does it prevent access to unwanted material?

Hardware and software requirements

☐ What operating system is required (for example, Windows or OS X)?

☐ What is the minimum memory and processor speed required?

☐ Is special hardware required such as a 3-D video card, a microphone, headphones, or a joystick?

Technical support

☐ Is the warranty sufficient?

☐ Are upgrades, or patches, available regularly, and, if so, what are the costs?

☐ Are response times acceptable should a problem occur?

Training

☐ What training is required for both the educator and the student?

☐ Are printed manuals required?

Coaching

- Remember, computers are tools, not educators. Educational software can be a valuable interactive lesson enhancement, but it should not replace a lesson. Preparation for computer time and then follow-up are important to the learning process.

- Consider alternative input devices such as touch screens, voice recognition devices, and child-size keyboards and buttons—especially for students with special needs.

- Avoid simplistic repetitive, or drill, software that demands one exact answer. Instead, the software should respond to wrong answers by giving new information that guides the user to the right answer, and new problems should be fresh and challenging.

- Not all educational software has to be lesson specific. Typical office software such as Word processing and slide shows can be educational when creatively employed.

Additional Reading

Editors of Children's Software Revue. n.d. Choosing children's software. Children's Technology Review. http://www.childrenssoftware.com/choosing.

Freeman, Nancy K., and Jennifer Somerindyke. 2001. Social play at the computer: Preschoolers scaffold and support peers' computer competence. *Information Technology in Childhood Education Annual*: 203–13.

Microweb.com/pepsite (URL no longer active).

Mobius Corporation Staff, eds. 1994. Computers in Head Start classrooms: Recommendations from the Head Start/IBM Partnership Project. 2nd ed. ERIC Digest ED394490.

Ra.terc.edu/SoftwareEval/SoftwareEvalHome.cfm (URL no longer active).

Spencer, Mima. 1986. Choosing software for children. ERIC Digest ED267914.

Starr, Linda. 2001. Load 'em up: The best software in the education world! Education World. http://www.education-world.com/a_tech/tech102.shtml.

SuperKids educational software reviews. http://www.superkids.com.

Wenglinsky, Harold. 1998. *Does it compute? The relationship between educational technology and student achievement in mathematics*. Policy information report. Princeton, NJ: Educational Testing Service Policy Information Center (September).

REFLECTION

Computers in the Early Childhood Classroom: How Much of a Good Thing?

By Stacia Emerson. Reprinted from *CEE*, May 2008.

In the past, the question regarding computers and early childhood education was, *Should* computers be allowed in the classroom? Now the question is, *How much* should computers be used in the classroom? The debate continues about whether computer use is beneficial or whether it is a health hazard for young children. The answer lies in how well the teacher knows the ages and the abilities of the children in the classroom. It is the teacher's responsibility to determine the best use of computers in the classroom. The teacher should evaluate classroom technology tools such as computers in order to determine whether they create the best possible learning situation for the students (Eliason and Jenkins 2003). Teachers should also take time to plan how they will integrate computers and other media into the curriculum.

The charts on the following pages give practical ways to ensure that the teacher is integrating various media in age-appropriate ways. One of the most important ideas is that the teacher should engage the students by asking questions about what they are experiencing on the screen.

If children are spending most of their time engaged in active, hands-on learning that promotes creative learning and problem solving, then technology such as computers can be an asset to the early childhood curriculum (Eliason and Jenkins 2003). For example, watching a DVD about ocean life should not take the place of going to the aquarium to view oceanic animals, examining shells in the science center, or reading books on the subject. But the information from the DVD can enhance the hands-on learning that has already taken place.

Threes

The children can ...	The teacher can ...
• tell simple stories	✓ ask specific questions about what is on TV or the computer; use the activities to expand the children's vocabulary usage
• sing simple songs	✓ choose computer activities and videos that include songs and rhythms; allow the children to sing and dance to the music
• name and match basic shapes and colors	✓ ask specific questions: What shape is that house? What color is that ball?
• distinguish between same and different	✓ point out likenesses and differences in characters on the screen; have the children copy the characters by, for example, asking the children to do simple motions
• ask who, what, why	✓ explain who characters are, what characters are doing, and why certain things happen
• move their bodies in new ways	✓ choose videos and computer activities that encourage moving, singing, and dancing

Fours

The children can ...	The teacher can ...
• understand and enjoy routines	✓ provide a consistent routine that includes TV and computer usage
• understand quantity, quality, and relationships: tall, big, more, on, in, above	✓ choose software and TV programs that reinforce concepts; talk about those concepts with the children
• have big imaginations	✓ allow the children to tell their version of the story or program they have seen even though they may exaggerate ✓ encourage the children to incorporate characters from books, shows, software, and other sources into their dramatic play ✓ make sure the children know which parts of a show or a story are real and which are make-believe
• understand and follow simple rules	✓ develop and enforce consistent rules regarding media use
• feel frustration and anger	✓ avoid stories that portray characters who use violence to solve conflicts

Fives

The children can ...	The teacher can ...
• like to make up games that have rules	✓ choose computer games that allow exploration or that allow the children to make choices such as what rules to set
• sort things by size and create groups of objects	✓ choose computer software that encourages the children to sort, match, count, and put things in sequences; point out groups during other activities
• like to argue and use the word *because*	✓ ask "what if" questions about TV shows and computer activities
• be very interested in cause and effect	✓ choose quality software that shows how things work; look for activities with sequences in which one event leads to another
• enjoy making up stories and know that stories have a beginning, a middle, and an end	✓ choose software programs that have prompts for creating stories; use word processing programs for publishing the children's stories; ask questions about the sequence of events in the stories

(Material adapted from PBS n.d.)

Consider the following principles for guidance regarding integrating computers into center-time activities (Day 1994):

- Computer activities should make learning *relevant* to the children's real-world situations. For example, computers should teach the children to solve problems and to communicate effectively with others.

- Computers should make learning *appealing*. Experiences with computers should get the children involved and should encourage them to be lifelong learners.

- Computers should provide *developmentally appropriate* learning. The concept development related to computer use should move from concrete, hands-on experiences to more abstract experiences and should depend on the children's developmental levels, learning styles, and interests.

- Computers should make learning *successful*. Each child should be able to see progress in learning through computers and should experience success.

Although computer screens look right at home nestled between the science and library centers, the question still remains regarding how much children should use computers in the classroom. The answer? It depends! It depends on each child's development, age, interest, and experience!

References

Day, Barbara D. 1994. *Early childhood education: Developmental experiential teaching and learning.* 4th ed. Upper Saddle River, NJ: Prentice Hall.

Eliason, Claudia, and Loa Jenkins. 2003. *A practical guide to early childhood curriculum.* 7th ed. Upper Saddle River, NJ: Prentice Hall.

PBS. n.d. Computers: Preschoolers. http://pbs.org/parents/childrenandmedia/computers-preschool.html.

REFLECTION

Examining the Technology Explosion: Do Computers Enhance or Detract from a Child's Growth and Development?

By Connie Mitchell. Reprinted from *CEE*, May 2008.

Maybe the approach by caregivers to children's computer use should reflect the approach of some caregivers to children's TV viewing. In my childhood home, my parents made choices about their children's television viewing. I remember the household TV rules for us kids:

- We could watch only for one hour a week.
- Although not a focal point of the living room, the TV was placed in such a way that everyone in the family could see and hear the programs. My mother almost always watched with us.
- We could watch only if we had finished our chores, homework, piano practice, and devotions.
- Although my parents listened to our requests and weighed the reviews of other parents, we could watch only shows such as *Howdy Doody* and *I Love Lucy* and only if those shows came on at appropriate times.
- We had to sit a distance from the screen and had to have lights on in the room.
- We had to turn off the TV if company came or if there were adult conversations taking place.
- My parents revoked TV privileges when we behaved inappropriately or exhibited inappropriate attitudes.

Fortunately, my parents also modeled watching TV appropriately, and they talked with us about biblical principles concerning the need to be careful of what we put into our minds, the need to use our time wisely, and the need to understand the importance of eternal values. As we grew older, we memorized verses that stay with me today:

- "Finally, brothers, whatever is true, whatever is noble, whatever is right, whatever is pure, whatever is lovely, whatever is admirable—if anything is excellent or praiseworthy—think about such things" (Philippians 4:8).
- " Be diligent to present yourself approved to God" (2 Timothy 2:15, NKJV).
- " For the things which are seen are temporary, but the things which are not seen are eternal" (2 Corinthians 4:18, NKJV).

Our family was one of the last families on the block to get a TV and was certainly one of the few to have rules. In some cases, my parents even individualized boundaries according to the child. Today, parents and teachers of young children face similar choices concerning computers.

Growth in Preschool Computer Use

Caregivers cannot ignore the increasing occurrence of computer technology. NCES statistics from 2001 assert that 90 percent of children and adolescents age 5 through 17 use computers and that 59 percent use the Internet. This use starts early: 75 percent of 5-year-olds use computers, and 25 percent of them use the Internet (DeBell and Chapman 2003, iv).

In the more recent *Kids and Consumer Electronics Trends III*, the NPD Group (2007) affirms that the average age at which children begin using electronic devices has declined from 8.1 years in 2005 to 6.7 years in 2007. The report states that the average age for children is 4 or 5, when they have their initial exposure to desktop computers. I have seen software advertised for babies who are as young as 9 months old. *LAPware* is promoted as a term for software that a young child uses while sitting in an adult's lap.

Questions

Endless questions come out of this technology explosion: At what age should children be exposed to computers at home or in the classroom? Do computers motivate children to learn faster and better? Must 5-year-olds receive training on computers today to get jobs in our technological society of tomorrow? Does technology encourage social isolation?

Understandably, parents and educators are apprehensive about the potential risks, wondering about the benefits of computer use by young children. Impassioned advocates for and against the use of technology by preschoolers continually debate the issues.

Point/Counterpoint: What Does the Research Say?

Supporters want children to have all the help that new technologies can bring to growth and learning. Proponents cite research on 3- and 4-year-olds who had significantly greater developmental gains, enhanced self-concept, and increasing levels of spoken communication and cooperation after computer use.

Critics are concerned about the shortcutting of the development process, the waste in time and money, the lure of commercialism, and the loss of childhood. A report issued by the Alliance for Childhood (2004), a child advocacy group, states that computers have not proved to have positive effects on children and that computers may be both physically and intellectually harmful.

Others focus on a middle-of-the-road approach, giving consideration to the individual needs of children. Northwest Educational Technology Consortium states that appropriately used technology "can be a positive factor in a child's learning process" but that two questions need to be considered when introducing a young child to technology: (1) "Is it developmentally appropriate—is it consistent with how a child develops and learns and with the child's current developmental stage?" and (2) "Will the activity benefit the child, or will it replace some other, more meaningful learning activities?" (NETC n.d.).

Realistically, choices have to be made about technology since it has or can become a common element in most children's lives. As with most trends in early childhood, technology use has come with an assortment of assumptions concerning development and learning. It is a provocative topic. Parents and teachers will need to research, study, use their experience, and look to God for wisdom to make decisions for each child and for each group of children. Let me suggest some resources that summarize issues and that discuss appropriate practice from some of the recent voices on this topic:

- In the book *The Power of Play*, child psychologist David Elkind (2007) writes a chapter on screen play and iconic literacy, providing guidance in using electronic media. He bases his guidance on individual differences and age appropriateness.

- In the book *Failure to Connect*, Jane M. Healy (1998) writes extensively on how computers affect children's minds. For 25 years, she was enthusiastic about the possibilities of computer use for learning, but she has since reversed her position.

- In "Less Screen Time, More Play Time," Edward Miller (2005) challenges the trend of introducing advanced technology into early childhood classrooms.

- The report *Fool's Gold*, published by the Alliance for Childhood, calls for a moratorium on the further introduction of computers in early childhood, except for special cases of students who have disabilities, until more research is conducted and improved strategies are in place (Cordes and Miller 2000). In the more recent publication *Tech Tonic*, the Alliance for Childhood (2004) offers 10 principles for developing technology literacy.

- In "Blackbox in the Sandbox," Rosemary Skeele and Gretchen Stefankiewicz (2002) refute the arguments made in *Fool's Gold* and support the decision to use technology with young children. The article provides an annotated bibliography of Internet resources for teachers.

- In "Strip Mining for Gold: *Research and Policy in Educational Technology—a Response to Fool's Gold*," Douglas Clements and Julie Sarama (2003) summarize research, delineate issues, and include their concerns about the use of computers.

- In "Technology in the Early Childhood Classroom," Elizabeth Hubbell (2007) examines how the nine categories of instructional strategies identified in *Classroom Instruction That Works* (Marzano, Pickering, and Pollock 2001) can help create significant learning experiences when used in conjunction with technology.

- The authors of "Beyond Gaming" (Hertzog and Klein 2005) and the authors of "Meaningful Connections" (Murphy, DePasquale, and McNamara 2003) share examples of how they have integrated technology into the curriculum.

- The Northwest Regional Educational Laboratory published a booklet that calls for finding a balance in using technology. The booklet reviews research and computer use in early childhood curricula (Van Scoter, Ellis, and Railsback 2001).

- *Early Childhood Today* (1999) asked, "Should young children have early access to computers?" to the following proponents of opposing views: Drs. Douglas Clements and Jane Healy. In the interview, Douglas Clements offers guidelines for computer use, and Jane Healy explains why she recommends that children under the age of 7 should not use computers.

- The National Association for the Education of Young Children (n.d.) presents a detailed position paper on technology and young children. The recommendations include emphasizing professional judgment, equitable access, collaboration with parents, professional development, and appropriate technology use as one option to support learning.

- The National Educational Technology Standards project is an ongoing initiative of the International Society for Technology in Education (ISTE). National standards have been developed for prekindergarten through second grade (ISTE 2000).

- Several online resources review children's software, including media for preschoolers. Although there is a subscription cost, Children's Technology Review (previously Children's Software Revue) has a searchable database that provides more than 7,000 software reviews and a print magazine (www.childrenssoftware.com). The free software review site, SuperKids, has a searchable database that rates software on the basis of education value, kid appeal, parent friendliness, and ease of use. SuperKids buyer's guide provides current market prices for PC and Mac software versions (www.superkids.com).

Personal Thoughts

If we are going to incorporate computers into the lives of children under the age of 5, it would seem that my parents' rules for television use could help shape our thinking today about computer use. Caregivers need to base their decisions on individual children's development and learning styles. Caregivers should limit children's computer use so that computers do not usurp the children's physical and socialization activities. Time limits can help prevent harmful effects, such as eye, back, and wrist strain. Computers should be in an area of the home or classroom where caregivers can easily observe and participate in their use. Caregivers should monitor computer content to prevent inappropriate imagery and information, as well as online interactions with strangers. Parents and schools should make use of media reviews and protective software. Training for parents and teachers should be available in technology, media literacy, and child development to ensure that the use of computers by children is effective and responsible. Discipline and good behavior should come first. Computers are not babysitters, and they should not substitute for human interaction. Since we live in era of the increasing availability of computer technology to babies, toddlers, and preschoolers, we as caregivers have an essential and critical role in guiding children in their use of computers.

References

Alliance for Childhood. 2004. *Tech tonic: Towards a new literacy of technology.* http://www.alliancefor childhood.org/projects/computers/pdf_files/tech_tonic.pdf.

Clements, Douglas H., and Julie Sarama. 2003. Strip mining for gold: Research and policy in educational technology—a response to "Fool's gold." *AACE Journal* 11, no. 1:7–69.

Cordes, Coleen, and Edward Miller, eds. 2000. *Fool's gold: A critical look at computers in childhood.* College Park, MD: Alliance for Childhood.

DeBell, Matthew, and Chris Chapman. 2003. *Computer and Internet use by children and adolescents in 2001: Statistical analysis report.* Washington, DC: National Center of Educational Statistics.

Early Childhood Today. 1999. ETC Interviews: Computers and young children. *Early Childhood Today* (October): 44–47. http://content.scholastic.com/browse/article.jsp?id=3745649.

Elkind, David. 2007. *The power of play: How spontaneous, imaginative activities lead to happier, healthier children.* Cambridge, MA: Da Capo Press.

Healy, Jane M. 1998. *Failure to connect: How computers affect our children's minds—and what we can do about it.* New York: Touchstone.

Hertzog, Nancy, and Marjorie Klein. 2005. Beyond gaming: A technology explosion in early childhood classrooms. *Gifted Child Today* 28, no. 3 (Summer): 24–31, 65.

Hubbell, Elizabeth Ross. 2007. Technology in the early childhood classroom. *Learning and Leading with Technology* (March): 32–35.

International Society for Technology in Education. 2000. *National educational technology standards for students: Connecting curriculum and technology.* Eugene, OR: International Society for Technology in Education.

ISTE. *See* International Society for Technology in Education.

Marzano, Robert J., Debra J. Pickering, and Jane E. Pollock. 2001. *Classroom instruction that works: Research-based strategies for increasing student achievement.* Alexandria, VA: Association for Supervision and Curriculum Development.

Miller, Edward. 2005. Less screen time, more play time: A new report challenges the trend for introducing advanced technology into early childhood classrooms. *Principal 85*, no. 1 (September/ October): 36–39.

Murphy, Karen, Roseanne DePasquale, and Erin McNamara. 2003. Meaningful connections: Using technology in primary classrooms. *Beyond the Journal* (November). http://www.journal.naeyc.org/ btj/200311/techinprimaryclassrooms.pdf.

National Association for the Education of Young Children. n.d. Technology and young children—ages 3 through 8. Position statement. http://www.naeyc.org/about/positions/PSTECH98.asp.

NETC. *See* Northwest Educational Technology Consortium.

Northwest Educational Technology Consortium. n.d. Early connections: Technology in early childhood education—children's development. http://www.netc.org/earlyconnections/index1.html.

NPD Group. 2007. Children are becoming exposed to and adopting electronic devices at earlier ages. Press release. (June 5). http://www.npd.com/press/releases/press_070605.html.

Skeele, Rosemary, and Gretchen Stefankiewicz. 2002. Blackbox in the sandbox: The decision to use technology with young children with annotated bibliography of Internet resources for teachers of young children. *Educational Technology Review* 10, no. 2:79–95.

Van Scoter, Judy, Debbie Ellis, and Jennifer Railsback. 2001. *Technology in early childhood education: Finding the balance.* Portland, OR: Northwest Regional Educational Laboratory.

Additional Reading

Shields, Margie K., and Richard E. Behrman. 2000. Children and computer technology: Analysis and recommendations. *Children and Computer Technology* 10, no. 2 (Fall/Winter). http://www .futureofchildren.org/pubs-info2825/pubs-info_show.htm?doc_id=69787.

REFLECTION

Section 5 Authors

The ACSI Technology Department supports Christian ministry worldwide through Web publishing, data processing and reporting, hardware and networking support, and help desk services. The department also lends a listening ear and does kitchen duty at ACSI's international headquarters.

Stacia Emerson, PhD, has served in multiple roles within early education: a teacher, a Sunday school teacher, and a college professor. She is currently a professor at Texas Wesleyan University.

D'Arcy Maher, MEd, serves as ACSI's director of Early Education Services. She is also the managing editor of *Christian Early Education* magazine.

Connie Mitchell, EdD, serves the College of Education at Columbia International University as associate dean for education programs. She has been teaching since 1967, almost entirely in biblical higher education. Although she has often had an administrative role, including many responsibilities with accreditation, Connie feels teaching in the classroom and at conferences is her most enjoyable role. She desires to support educators in their quest to serve as teachers and educational leaders, sustained with a Christian philosophy of education and a global vision. When not teaching, Connie enjoys traveling with her husband, George.

Section 6:
Bonus Articles

Stumped About Summer? Ideas to Promote Learning

By Tom Sweigard and Kaitlin Sattler. Reprinted from *CEE*, March 2008.

Summer has begun, and children are soaking up the sun and playing outside with all their friends. Mrs. Babb—the mother of Laura, age seven, and Josh, age three—watches her children play as she sorts through the papers that came home during the last week of school. In the stack she finds a suggested reading list for Laura, and Mrs. Babb sighs as she foresees the battle that will ensue when she tries encouraging Laura to read at least one of the books on the list or even to spend time reading aloud to Josh. "Not today," Mrs. Babb thinks to herself. "I'll have them start working on it next week." But each week, she pushes it off one more week, trying to avoid any conflict with her children.

Allowing the reading list to collect dust during the summer is a common response of parents who have children who are uninterested in reading, but it is not an appropriate one because it allows students to ignore this important time of growth for an entire three months. Studies have shown that students who do not read or who are not read to during the summer months are prone not only to losing some of the reading ability they gained the year before but also to falling behind their peers academically, especially in reading. Researchers call this phenomenon "summer reading loss." It is a critical issue in education today, causing academic growth to slow to a virtual standstill in some students and causing academic regression in others. Studies have blamed part of the achievement gap on this specific issue (Mraz and Rasinski 2007).

The efforts of parents and teachers can reduce the achievement gap caused by summer reading loss. What can you as parents do now with your preschoolers to prevent this problem at a later time? What learning opportunities and experiences will help your children have a positive attitude toward reading and a desire to read for pleasure?

Children who read regularly or who are otherwise exposed to good literature develop a larger vocabulary and better comprehension skills that will help them not only to read more fluently but also to communicate effectively and understand content areas more easily than do their peers (Tompkins 2007). Students who read as few as three or four books or hear books read to them can reap tremendous benefits and improve their reading proficiency in only a few months (Kim 2004).

Literacy Development in Young Children

Literacy growth, necessary to reading development in children, could actually begin before birth because babies can remember music and voices they hear while in the womb. After birth, infants continue to develop their literacy skills by listening to those around them speak. They then experiment with their ability to speak the language of adults by cooing and babbling (Lawhon and Cobb 2002). These listening and speaking skills make up a vital literacy-development step that helps young children understand the connection between spoken language and written text.

Environmental Print

The sign that reads "Wal-Mart" above the door to the store, the label "Crest" on the toothpaste tube, and the words "Fruity Pebbles" on the cereal box—these are instances of environmental print: words and symbols that children regularly see in the world around them (Tompkins 2007).

By the time young children begin to use complete thoughts or phrases in their communication, they are already beginning to understand the relationship between the print they see in the environment and the meaning it has (Bowman and Treiman 2004). Riding through a town around dinnertime, many two-year-olds will recognize the "Golden Arches" as McDonald's. As part of emerging literacy, this stage identifies the period when children begin to comprehend the importance of written language. Once they begin to make such connections, they will then be able to understand the alphabet and connect each letter with the sound it creates. Emergent readers depend on context to be able to read and memorize texts. Following this stage, children will begin to take meaning from letter groupings and words. This is the beginning of the formal reading process.

Understanding the Process and Identifying Activities

Understanding the process of literacy development in young children is critical for parents who want to help their children learn to read well because it allows parents to select activities and experiences that encourage reading. In order to help parents identify activities and experiences that are beneficial to literacy development in children, researchers have studied which methods and programs work best for young children. Library story times help children develop their literacy skills, print awareness, alphabetic knowledge, and familiarity with a variety of literary genres.

Library Access

Children who frequently access library materials are noted to have a stronger interest in reading than their peers who do not go to the library as often (Kim 2004). When children go to the library regularly, they have access to multitudes of books that interest them and have a routine activity that they can eagerly anticipate. Children who have much experience with books, in any context, have a high probability of becoming excellent readers (Scarborough, Dobrich, and Hager 1991).

Parent Expectations

Maybe somewhat surprising, one of the most noted encouragements for literacy development is the expectations of parents. Parents who model excellent reading habits and create a home atmosphere in which reading is enjoyed and respected are more likely to instill in their children a passion for reading. Generally, students respond well to these expectations, pursuing reading as a pleasurable activity (Kim 2004).

Things You Are Probably Already Doing!

To encourage literacy growth, parents and other caregivers can use many practical ideas that are based on the language development of young children:

- **Read aloud.** Make reading to your children a daily routine beginning in the first days of their lives. As you read together, show your children the end pages and title pages, and point out familiar letters in the text. Ask your children to read any repeated sections. This reading time will introduce your children to book concepts and will help them develop a love for reading (Tompkins 2007).

- **Incorporate words into play activities.** Many young children play "house" or do similar activities that copy what adults do. Provide your children with books, old cookbooks, coupons, magazines, or anything else that has print. Children emulate what adults do, and they will use the props you give them and thus will practice using oral and written language (Janisch 2003).

- **Talk about print as you go about everyday activities.** While eating breakfast with your children, point out the words on the back of the cereal box. Point to signs on the road as you drive places with your children. Help your children identify letters on food items in the grocery store. These simple activities will help your children understand the value of print and will encourage them to make connections between spoken and written language.

- **Color and write.** Through coloring, children are taking a step toward developing their ability to write. Give them crayons and paper, and let them practice making print. While on vacation, ask your children to color pictures of what they see or to write words describing the activities they do.

- **Go to the library with your children.** Most libraries have story time or other programs for both school-age children and preschool children (Hughes-Hassell, Agosto, and Sun 2007). Take regular trips to the library, as mentioned above, and go to local bookstores. Make these visits fun outings that your children will want to do. Don't underestimate the importance of these family trips.

- **Set expectations.** Create a home atmosphere that treasures reading, and model to your children the importance of reading by reading books aloud to your children and making sure that the books are appropriate for their reading level. Also, be a reader yourself !

In Conclusion

The establishment of routines that promote literacy growth in the beginning years of life is critical to the development of young children. Activities that promote print awareness are simple and fun to experience with your children. You do not have to face years of battling with your children about summer reading assignments. Helping your children appreciate excellent literature is an important process and an achievable goal. As you incorporate reading into your children's lives, your children will begin to appreciate not only the value of reading but also the summer routines of going to the library and bookstores with you.

Mrs. Babb and her children, Laura and Josh, experienced a wonderful summer together. There were family vacations, swimming lessons, lazy days, and fun trips to the local library. These trips to return and collect new treasures from the library, as well as the family's nightly read-aloud times, motivated the family to share in the appreciation of good literature and reading.

Celebrate good literature for young children for the benefit of literacy development and reading growth as well as for sheer enjoyment. What could be better than reading a good book—such as the classic *Goodnight Moon*—in the car, at the beach, or at bedtime after a fun, relaxing summer day? Turn off the TV, have fun, and read!

References

Bowman, Margo, and Rebecca Treiman. 2004. Stepping stones to reading. *Theory into Practice* 43, no. 4 (Autumn): 295–303.

Hughes-Hassell, Sandra, Denise E. Agosto, and Xiaoning Sun. 2007. Making storytime available to children of working parents: Public libraries and the scheduling of children's literacy programs. *Children and Libraries* 5, no. 2 (Summer/Fall): 43–48.

Janisch, Carole. 2003. The hurried child then and now: What this means for learning and literacy development. *International Journal of Social Education* 18, no 1 (Spring/Summer): 24–34.

Kim, Jimmy. 2004. Summer reading and the ethnic achievement gap. *Journal of Education for Students Placed at Risk* 9, no. 2 (April): 169–88.

Lawhon, Tommie, and Jeanne B. Cobb. 2002. Routines that build emergent literacy skills in infants, toddlers, and preschoolers. *Early Childhood Education Journal* 30, no. 2 (Winter): 113–18.

Mraz, Maryann, and Timothy V. Rasinski. 2007. Summer reading loss. *Reading Teacher* 60, no. 8:784–89.

Scarborough, Hollis S., Wanda Dobrich, and Maria Hager. 1991. Preschool literacy experience and later reading achievement. *Journal of Learning Disabilities* 24, no. 8 (October): 508–11.

Tompkins, Gail E. 2007. *Literacy for the 21st century: Teaching reading and writing in prekindergarten through grade 4.* 2nd ed. Upper Saddle River, NJ: Pearson Education.

REFLECTION

Warning! Unleashing Creativity Can Energize Your Classroom

By Stacia Emerson. Reprinted from *CEE*, May 2009.

Sometimes, words we hear and use frequently are not easy to define. For instance, what exactly do *creative*, *create*, and *imagination* mean—all of which relate to the concept of creativity? A search in the *Merriam-Webster Online Dictionary* reveals the following:*

- *Creative* (adjective): marked by the ability or power to create
- *Create* (verb): to produce through imaginative skill
- *Imagination* (noun): the act or power of forming a mental image of something not present to the senses or never before wholly perceived in reality

A textbook definition of *creativity* is "the process of developing original, high-quality, genuinely significant products" (Spodek and Saracho 1994, 452). Even though creativity may be an elusive concept, it is an idea that you as early childhood teachers are familiar with. There has been much discussion about ways to increase creativity and creative problem-solving skills in young children. For children to develop fully in specific areas, they need time, materials, and opportunity to practice. You can encourage creativity and imagination in young children by doing the following:

Accepting original ideas. An environment that encourages children to share their ideas and create original products will enhance creativity. Create this environment by not focusing on one right answer to a question and not expecting all paintings or collages to look the same. If you communicate to children that their ideas are valued and that they are competent, then those children will be more likely to take risks and try new things.

Providing opportunities for children to discover the world around them through their senses. Even though children make sense of their world through their senses, the experiences they have should be more than just isolated sensory activities (Spodek and Saracho 1994). Activities such as those using shakers and texture blocks give children valuable developmental experience. But these are isolated events. Allowing children to experience sights, sounds, and smells as they do activities such as digging a garden patch or feeding ducks incorporates their sensory learning into real-life situations. That incorporation is similar to applying spelling skills while writing a descriptive story.

Allowing plenty of time for children to interact with the environment. Children can interact with their environment by using their senses, by talking with others, or by thinking about an experience (Spodek and Saracho 1994). Simply observing the environment is not enough. Children need time to interact and respond.

Providing quality materials. The materials offered in the early childhood classroom should extend children's possibilities, not limit those possibilities (Spodek and Saracho 1994). It is frustrating to children when they paint with watery, dull paint and thin paper that tears from the least pressure. Make sure that the materials you provide—such as paper, paint, crayons, markers, and clay—are quality materials. Also keep in mind that it is not the product itself that measures the success of the activity. It is the process. Paper that tears or dough that is dry and crumbly will not encourage children to return to that activity over and over.

Keeping the above guidelines in mind, choose specific activities such as the following that can encourage creative development:

Infants

- Play various types of music during routines.
- Sing songs to infants and move to the rhythm.
- Provide complex items for infants to observe such as mobiles, banners, photographs, and aquariums.
- Read books that include interesting illustrations.
- Provide appropriate toys for sensory exploration.

Two-Year-Olds

- Continue with above activities.
- Teach fingerplays, and allow children to imitate movements.
- Provide fat crayons or nontoxic markers for children to use for scribbling

on various papers, making sure you closely supervise the children. Start with one crayon or marker for each child.

- Provide play dough and plastic utensils—a combination that gives children many opportunities for problem solving and creativity. Keep in mind that teacher-made play dough has a better consistency for younger preschoolers than does manufacturer-made play dough.

Three- and Four-Year-Olds

- Use the same materials listed above but in more complex ways. Give children more colors of markers or crayons or more utensils with the play dough.

- Provide a variety of collage materials—such as torn paper, stickers, pipe cleaners, nature items, magazine pictures, and old greeting cards—for open-ended exploration.

- Use unconventional materials for exploration to open children's minds to the possibility of new uses for everyday materials. For example, use markers to draw on aluminum foil or paper plates, and make books from stapled paper plates or lunch sacks.

- Start a collection of materials—such as cardboard tubes, oatmeal containers, coffee containers, small boxes, plastic lids, and craft sticks—for children to use for creating. Ask the children to help with the collection, and allow plenty of time for them to build.

Use these activities as a starting point to encouraging creativity in the classroom, but by all means use *your* imagination to keep adding to the list!

Note

Merriam-Webster Online Dictionary, s.vv. "creative," http://www.merriam-webster.com/dictionary/creative; "create," http://www.merriamwebster.com/dictionary/create; "imagination," http://www.merriam-webster.com/dictionary/imagination (accessed February 16, 2009).

Reference

Spodek, Bernard, and Olivia N. Saracho. 1994. *Right from the start: Teaching children ages three to eight.* Needham Heights, MA: Allyn and Bacon.

REFLECTION

Top 10 Qualities of Christian Early Educators

Compiled by Julia Wurst.
Reprinted from the ACSI Early Education Conference Journal, August 2010.

1. *Jesus-like:* Christ's example with and teaching on children must infuse every interaction, reflecting God's intense delight in children through personal, individualized interactions that show deeply interested and sensitive adults.

2. *Encouraging:* Young children need affirmation from the adults in their lives as they discover how to live, move, and learn.

3. *Flexible:* Childhood is seen and honored as a God-ordained process characterized by unique and distinct development.

4. *Creative:* Fostering a culture of curiosity creates an environment of never-ending ideas and discovery that encourages children to be intentional participants in all areas of life.

5. *Loving:* The second-greatest commandment is to love one another. Being an example of love creates stability that has lifelong effects in children's lives.

6. *Patient:* Development is not hurried or left to chance. Experiences that will be meaningful for the age levels in each classroom are intentionally planned.

7. *Mature:* Biblical principles that are expressed in teachers' lives, not isolated in the curriculum, become alive and are transmitted effectively.

8. *Sensitive:* Christian early education teachers strive to interact with children and families in the same way that Christ would if He were serving in that program.

9. *Teachable* (a lifelong learner): Adults who continually learn promote continuous learning in children. Children in a community of learners gain appreciation for cultures, gender, and differently abled students because the adult leaders place individual value on each child.

10. *Quick to listen:* Children need to know that both your ears and your eyes value their words, thoughts, and ideas. Seeking first to understand and then to be understood is a humble posture that shows parents that you respect them as their children's primary teachers.

Section 6 Authors

Stacia Emerson, PhD, has served in multiple roles within early education: a teacher, a Sunday school teacher, and a college professor. She is currently a professor at Texas Wesleyan University.

Kaitlin Sattler is pursuing a bachelor's degree in multiage special education. Her love for reading began at a very young age when her mother read children's stories to her every afternoon. After finishing her bachelor's degree, Kaitlin would like to pursue a master's degree in elementary education or library science. In her free time, she enjoys reading, running, making music, and creating memories with people of all ages.

Tom Sweigard, PhD, is an associate professor and an early childhood education coordinator at Cedarville University in Cedarville, Ohio. Having always loved school, he naturally became an elementary teacher. He has taught all levels, from kindergarten classes through graduate courses over a 38-year career in education. He is married to his childhood sweetheart, Patti, and they have three children and two grandchildren. Tom loves teaching, music, gardening, bike riding, reading, and spending time with his family at their summer cottage in Lakeside, Ohio, on Lake Erie.

Julia Wurst, BA, serves as ACSI's Media Specialist for Early Education Services. She is also the associate editor for *Christian Early Education* magazine.

REFLECTION

Action Plans/Reflections

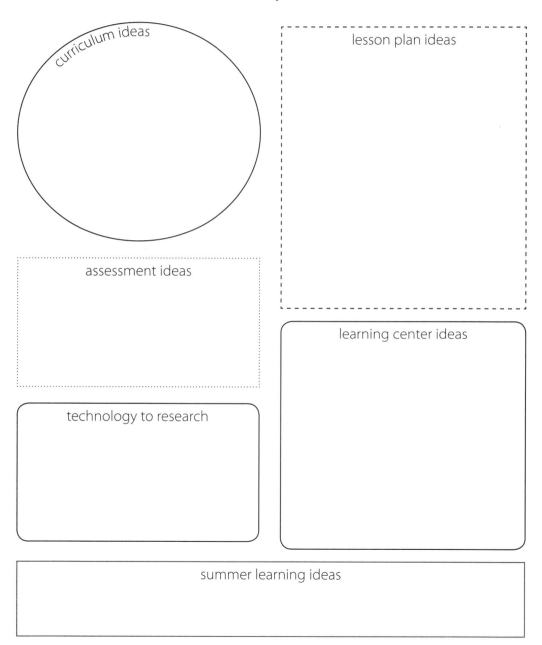

curriculum ideas

lesson plan ideas

assessment ideas

learning center ideas

technology to research

summer learning ideas

communicate to parents

classroom changes

share with director

center ideas

ideas to encourage creativity

other ideas

Other Resources from Purposeful Design Products

Cultivate, Nurture, Grow: The Spiritual Development of Young Children

The spiritual development of young children is the core ministry of early educators. This resource unlocks the mystery of spiritual development with new content, articles from *Christian Early Education*, and a bonus CD of materials.

Preschool Associate Credential Manual

This manual takes the applicant step-by-step through the process of achieving the Preschool Associate Credential. It thoroughly outlines the education, observation, and portfolio components of the credential requirements. All necessary forms along with the application are included.

Supporting Families Through Meaningful Ministry

This resource is designed to strengthen your connection with the families of the children in your classroom and programs. It includes articles from *Christian Early Education*, a family evaluation tool, parent pages to augment your own newsletter, and parent education ideas. A bonus CD of materials is also included!

Professional Growth for Early Educators

This CD fulfills two roles: it can be used by a teacher interested in aggressively developing professionally, or it can also be used by a director as part of the mentoring and annual review process of her team..

Early Education Director's Manual

This completely revised edition has over 250 pages of practical, insightful information on how to operate an effective early education center. It also includes a CD of customizable forms.

Now Tell It to Me: Using Retelling for Literacy and Language Development

This practical resource for early educators and primary-level teachers presents the use of retelling as a literacy and language development instructional strategy. The author provides many examples of how this tool can provide a solid foundation toward the development of excellent reading and language skills in students.

To order these products, contact ACSI Customer Service—phone: 800-367-0798, fax: 719-531-0716; or visit our online store at www.purposefuldesign.com.